PUB SIGNS

PAUL CORBALLIS

PUB SIGNS

PAUL CORBALLIS

Lennard Publishing
1988

Lennard Publishing
a division of Lennard Books Ltd

Lennard House
92 Hastings Street
Luton, Beds LU1 5BH

British Library Cataloguing in Publication Data

Corballis, Paul T.
Pub signs
1. England. Pub signs
I. Title
659.13'42

ISBN 1-85291-018-6

First published 1988
© Paul Corballis 1988

Phototypeset in Great Britain
by Jigsaw, Romford

Book Design by Pocknell and Co.

Reproduced, printed and bound in Great Britain

Contents

Introduction

7

Chapter 1: The Origins of Pubs and Pub Signs

10

Chapter 2: The Pub Sign in London

22

Chapter 3: Pub Sign Artists of the Past

39

Chapter 4: Today's Pub Sign Artists

69

Chapter 5: The Funny Side of the Sign

85

Chapter 6: History Lives on Signs –

an Explanation of Pub Names

89

Chapter 7: The Best in Britain

145

Bibliography and Acknowledgements

156

Index

158

A remarkably fine Victorian pub but it is a sight that would be unthinkable today, because it has no sign whatsoever, The Brondesbury Arms, Kilburn, in 1880.

INTRODUCTION

An introduction usually tells the reader why a book has been written
and a bit about what it will say. This introduction will also say a bit about
what this book is not. Before that, two quotations will enjoyably set the
scene.

William Cowper said:

> 'Not more distinct from harmony divine
> the constant creaking of a country sign'

And Ben Johnson:

> 'It even puts Apollo
> To all his strength of art to follow
> The flights, and to divine
> What's meant by every sign.'

This is a book about pub signs, written because of the pleasure they
give and because of their uniqueness in the worlds of art and commerce. It is
written to share that pleasure with others, to bring some recognition and
encouragement to the mostly anonymous artists who paint these original
works.

A pub sign's first job is to identify the premises as a pub. That function
could be fulfilled these days by a simple lettered sign such as those used by
the butcher, the baker and the greengrocer. But a pub sign has a wonderful
tradition of doing its job in a way that gives a personality, a face, to the pub it
represents, of doing its job through the medium of art and frequently with
humour. Pub signs don't represent a necessity of life, as do other trade signs.
Rather, they introduce one of life's greater pleasures. And just as British pubs
are unique in the world of drinking (and eating and socializing)
establishments, so too are pub signs. Occasionally, there are pictorial signs
outside bars in other countries, but they always seem to be a deliberate effort
to be different and rather arch, because pub signs are not a normal tradition
in that country.

A pub sign in the centre of London is probably seen by more people, in
its 10 years or so of useful life, than a painting by J. M. W. Turner in the Tate
Gallery. The difference is, of course, that people go to the Tate to *look* at a
Turner, to think about it and enjoy its beauty. All of Great Britain's roads,
streets and lanes are a Tate Gallery for pub signs. There is an unbelievable
profusion of art by countless artists just waiting there for us to *look* at and
enjoy.

This is not a book about beer. And it is not about pubs. Both of those
are essential to the story of pub signs and much of their history is briefly told,
but always as a backdrop to the signs and their artists. Because of this, the
word pub is used throughout the book in places where perhaps tavern or inn
or hotel could be more precise. And publican for the most part takes the
place of landlord, tenant, manager, free house owner and so on. For a slightly
different reason, 'beer' is used to represent all of the past and present
beverages available in a pub, since the words ale and beer have meant
different things in different centuries and since that is a subject very well
discussed in any number of books on beer and pubs. This book is not about
painting techniques, brush strokes or types of paint and varnish. It is more of
an appreciation of pub sign art than a 'how to' or technical discussion and
analysis.

While every effort has been made to be factual, that is not always possible with a subject so full of folklore and oral history. This is particularly true when talking about the origin of pub names and the reasons why pub signs show the pictures they do. If the reader disagrees with any explanation – or has a better story – the author would be delighted to hear from you. In a similar vein, the listing of attractive and interesting signs throughout Great Britain is very much a compilation of information from many people, many

Four photographs illustrate the evolution of the signs at one pub. The Holly Bush is a delightful pub situated on a country lane in Potters Crouch, near St Albans. In the last century, as shown in this picture, it was a rough, farmers' pub with its own stables attached to the right of the pub. It was then owned by the Chesham Brewery which placed its name first on the sign. Then, in big letters 'Fine Ales' and finally at the bottom, almost as an afterthought, The Holly Bush. This photo was taken around the turn of the century and also illustrates the growing literacy of the people – it proudly used only words, no pictorial.

Some 20–30 years later, the Holly Bush had added some rooms to the rear, dressed up the entranceway and whitewashed the brickwork. Chesham Brewery was now part of Benskins (which became a part of Ind Coope). While the pub now boasted fine Ales and Stout and, in smaller letters, wines and spirits, it also featured teas, a sign of changing times. The pub sign was now a pictorial one, confident enough of its own clarity that it did not name the pub. The painting showed the giant holly bush which grew nearby and had given the pub its name.

Another 20 years or so and the pub now had a smooth white finish and the stables had been turned into toilets. The pub sign was again a painting of a holly bush but this time a fat, squat one, not related to the bush

sources. Your favourites would be valuable for future revised or companion editions.

One more quotation to end with. It is about the pub and without the pub as described, there would be no pub sign.

'No, sir, there is nothing which has yet been contrived by man, by which so much happiness is produced as by a good tavern or inn'.

Samuel Johnson

8

behind the pub. Again it was clearly a holly bush and didn't have to have the name. Only the brewery name is on the sign.

By the late 1960s, the Holly Bush was rendered all the way back and had two pub signs, one on the front and one on the side. Going a step further from the original bush, this time the holly bush was a stylized one, attractive in a design sense but lacking the landscape painting appeal of the two former signs.

Chapter 1

THE ORIGINS OF PUBS AND PUB SIGNS

The story of pub signs naturally follows, and is part of, the story of pubs themselves. In turn, the story of pubs is part of the much larger and older story of beer. Beer, in fact, may be as old as – and indeed may be the cause of – civilization itself! That may seem hard to believe at first but it is the theory of at least one prominent anthropologist. Dr Solomon H. Katz, a Professor of Anthropology at the University of Pennsylvania in the United States, believes that beer is why people first settled down and began sowing, reaping and cultivating some 10,000 years ago. In an interview with *The New York Times* he said that prehistoric people accidentally discovered that wild wheat and barley soaked in water and left in the air did not spoil. Instead, the natural yeast in the air converted it to a dark, bubbling brew that made anyone drinking it feel good. It was also full of protein and it made people healthy. Dr Katz explains that this was enough to make the hunter-gatherers begin to cultivate crops and that this, in turn, led to settling in one place and the beginnings of community life.

Dr Katz's theories will undoubtedly be argued for years by anthropologists. But however and whenever it started, beer was a staple long before we began to record history. There have been many scientific and anthropological discoveries clearly proving the importance of beer and other alcoholic beverages in the centuries before the birth of Christ. In the Heineken Brewery Museum in Holland there is a sacrificial carving dated 3200–3000 BC, found at Sakkara, south of Cairo. It shows a person pouring a liquid and it is inscribed, 'filling the stone bottles with beer'. A tablet in the British Museum mentions beerhouses near Babylon about 2200 BC. In the fourteenth century BC, beer was known to be the favourite beverage of the Egyptians. Of course, one reason that beer was such a staple beverage before the birth of Christ and for centuries afterwards was simply that it was safer and healthier to drink than water.

Beer, then, is the first part of the background of the story. Pubs are the second and it is here that the Romans are important. It is certain that the Romans knew beer, although wine was much more their drink. In all of their

The Bush Called the Bush in a fourteenth-century manuscript, this is actually an ale-stake.

communities they established '*Tabernae*' (from which we get tavern), a place where wine was sold to be enjoyed on the premises or taken away. They also had more elaborate inns called '*Mansio*', which means house of rest. These were larger, with rooms for eating and drinking, resting and, sometimes, bathing. As the excavations in Pompeii showed, all Roman commercial establishments had identifying, pictorial or representational signs. And it is here that the story of pub signs really begins.

When the Romans came and occupied Britain after AD 43, they naturally brought with them their customs and ideas from other parts of their Empire. These included their *tabernae* or wine shops which sold wine for consumption on the premises. It is believed that these forerunners of the pub were built at regular intervals along their straight roads but this has never been proven, because none has been excavated archaeologically. The one possible exception was a hut beside the old road under Silbury Hill. Remains of rushes were found on the floor with some small coins buried under them making it appear that this was some kind of wayside eating or drinking house. It is, however, not Roman but built sometime later. The Roman *tabernae* would be even more likely to have been built in the shopping centres of their settlements.

Three modern pub signs can be traced directly to the Romans and their signs of commerce. The first of these, and the best known, is the Bush. This was the sign of the *taberna*, a bundle of grapevine leaves hung on a chain on the outside wall to indicate that new wine had been delivered and was ready for sale. Through the ensuing centuries to the present time there have been pubs called the Bush and using a version of this sign. Loosely related to the Bush in coming eras were the Ale-Stake, the Ale-Garland and indirectly (and often incorrectly) the Holly Bush. More of these as we come to them in time.

The Romans also first used the Chequers as a sign, one that is still popular today. Chequers signs were found in Pompeii. The Romans used the Chequers sign as a symbol for games like chess and draughts and it would be displayed outside a *taberna* to show that games could be played there. In Hogarth's eighteenth-century 'Beer St.', you can see a chequerboard fixed to the outside wall of a pub, separate from the pub sign. The popularity of the Chequers as a pub sign today can be equally traced to two other influences. Merchants and moneychangers did their business on chequered boards and used the board as a kind of abacus. The word 'exchequer' is descended from this. Later, the Earls of Warrenne were given the privilege and responsibility of licensing ale-houses in the Middle Ages and their escutcheon was a blue and gold chequerboard.

Because the traditional style of painting is so directly similar, we can say that the Two Brewers or Jolly Brewers is a direct descendant of a Roman sign. The Roman sign for a vintner showed two slaves carrying an amphora of wine suspended on a pole between them. The modern version shows two brewers carrying a barrel of beer suspended from a pole between them.

As time moved forward, there were three evolving practices that determined the shape of today's pubs and pub signs both stylistically and traditionally.

The Roman Legions left Britain in the fifth century and the following five hundred years saw successive invasions of Angles, Saxons and Danes. The Saxons were already ale drinkers. In fact, the word ale comes from the Saxon '*ealu*' and the Danish '*ol*'. They also introduced the Ale-Stake, a wooden pole driven into the thatch of a roof or planted upright in the ground to show that there was ale to be bought at that house. The end of the ale-stake would have a bundle of leaves, like the Roman Bush. Another pub word which comes from the Saxon is 'inn' which originally meant simply a room or chamber. Only later did inn come to mean a place where people could stay.

Every Saxon woman learned to brew, just as she learned to bake, from her mother and a woman who could not brew or bake was not considered much use as a wife! The word brewster is a feminine noun, from the Saxon, and even today the annual licensing sessions by the Justices which are held in February or March are called Brewster Sessions.

The ale-house developed naturally from one wife being a better brewster than the other wives in a settlement. She would sell her surplus rather than throw it away. In time, her hut would become the place where people went to drink ale, talk and relax and where passing trade would stop. In good weather, people would sit on a bench outside. But in poor weather, the drinkers would crowd into the one-room hut and gather round the cooking fire. This practice continued even after huts became larger and had more rooms. It is the forerunner of the public bar, where locals can gather in their working clothes and relax. If there were important guests or if guests were willing to pay a bit extra, they would be invited into the cleaner, better rooms. These eventually evolved into the saloon bar of today.

As one house in the community became the place to get ale, the Ale-Stake became identified with that house, became its pub sign. The house didn't need a name, just the identification that this was a place where ale could be bought. The practice of setting up an ale stake continued for centuries, sometimes with leaves or vines on the end, sometimes just with bristles. Sometimes it was elaborated with a garland attached. The Ale-Stake also started the tradition of pub signs hanging from a pole projecting out from the side of the pub or being on top of free-standing poles stuck in the ground in front of the pub.

By the beginning of the eighteenth century, the houses in the communities where people went to meet, to eat and to drink and relax, began to be called by a name we know today in a shorter, more familiar form. That ale-house began to be described as the Public House because it was for the use of all the public. Today we more commonly say Pub but the full name is still Public House. And it is much more than just a name. Pubs are intended to be and are open to all the public, with some minimum age restrictions. That tradition – being open to all the public – is combined with the other half of its name, 'house', to shape the character of the pubs and to help explain why they are unique in the world. The pub *is* a house and it is the home of the publican and his family. They treat the public as guests in their house and the public acts as guests. The centuries of tradition shaping this host-guest relationship and the fact that in the rest of the world, bars (by whatever name they are called) are not normally in or part of homes, is the keystone to understanding this unique British institution.

An indication that the Ale-Stake continued as a symbol or sign into the Middle Ages was its inclusion in the Bayeux Tapestry. In that part of the tapestry which depicts a house on fire, with the inscription '*Hic domus incenditur*', there is a large building next to it. Projecting from that building is a version of a pole and bush, the Ale-Stake. As this practice of having an identifying symbol continued and evolved through the centuries, a parallel development was taking place.

The church had an important rôle in the history of drinking establishments. As the centuries passed and abbeys and churches, monasteries and cathedrals were built throughout the land, another tradition of hosts and guests was developing. Traveller and pilgrims as well as official and unofficial visitors to these religious institutions had to be provided with food, drink and a place to sleep. At the same time, the workers building and

Two fourteenth-century depictions of inns, showing the sign of **The Golden Cross**.

maintaining these religious buildings (great or ordinary) needed places to get their food and beer. So either attached to them or nearby, public houses (called inns, from the Saxon) with accommodation were built and maintained by the religious hosts. Their signs showed pilgrims, visitors and workers where the pub could be found, and they naturally tended to depict religious symbols or themes such as the Seven Stars (in the crown of Mary), the Cross, the Crossed Keys (of the Kingdom of God) and later the Bull (from '*bulla*' an ecclesiastical seal) and the Pope's head. After Henry VIII broke with Rome, many such pubs kept the same name (or changed it slightly: the Pope's Head became the King's Head) but they changed the sign enough to go from religious to secular meaning.

The third influence on pubs and pub signs was also developing. With the development of large estates by the landed gentry, the estate workers, just like the lay workers in the religious communities, were supplied with beer as part of their wages and rations. These great estates normally established a house on the property and a brewster to prepare and serve the beer to the workers. At first (like the ale-house) this needed no name because everyone on the estate knew it was the public house. It might acquire a name or nickname from the work done nearby (the Plow, Harrow or Shears) or animals there (the Cow, Cock or Fox) or some feature of the land (the Oak Tree, Holly Bush or Vines). But, again, it also would serve as a resting place for visitors to the estate and travellers. Because of this it would need a sign to identify it and that sign might either be the name it was commonly called or the coat of arms or some heraldic device of the lord of the land. This was also true of ordinary ale-houses just outside the estate boundaries but perhaps built on land owned by the local lord or when the brewster owed some duty to the lord.

For example, near Berkhamsted, in Hertfordshire, is Ashridge, once a beautiful estate and now a National Trust property and open to the public. At the centre of the property is Ashridge House, a magnificent building which is now a management college but once served as the residence of the child who became Queen Elizabeth I. In three communities surrounding Ashridge, Berkhamsted, Frithsden and Little Gaddesden, there are three pubs with this kind of heritage, named after families associated with Ashridge House – the Brownlow Arms, the Alford Arms and the Bridgewater Arms. In each case, their signs depict the coat of arms of the family named.

The influences on the development of pubs and their signs of the Saxon ale-house, the religious guest house and the estate pubs were evolutionary and it would be difficult or impossible to put exact dates to each development. But there have also been influences which can be dated because they were official. While their specific effects have faded with the centuries, their influence is still part of the pub and pub sign story.

Today's often confusing licensing laws are not a modern invention but can be traced back at least as far as King Edgar (AD 959–975) who limited ale-houses to one per village or small town and established a standard for drink. And even the great Magna Carta did not ignore drink. It decreed, 'Let there be one measure of wine throughout our realm and one measure of ale'.

The first great proclamation to affect the future of pictorial pub signs throughout the realm came in 1393. King Richard II decreed that pubs, unlike any other trade or commercial establishment, must have signs, 'Whosoever shall brew ale in the town (London) with the intention of selling it must hang out a sign; otherwise he shall forfeit his ale'. This was done so that the ale-conner would know the location of each pub. He was an examiner or tester of ales and was appointed to oversee the quality and measures of ale being sold. The Ale-Garland, mentioned earlier as a direct descendant of the Bush, was hung on the sign whenever a new brew was ready for the ale-conner to test. The ale-garland was not a sign in itself in those days but always an addition to a sign. Later, the garland was often incorporated in the design of the sign or a stylized version of it became part of the ironwork. Today there are some pubs named the Ale-Garland. From the days of Richard II pubs and their signs became synonymous. Another passage of the law provided that everyone would know when a pub had lost its licence by its sign being taken down.

By 1375 there were so many pubs and pub signs in London that they were becoming a menace to traffic. An ordinance was passed stating that no pub should have an ale-stake bearing its sign or leaves projecting or extending over the King's highway more than seven feet at the utmost.

Once again in 1553 there was an attempt to limit the number of pubs to one per town, with certain exceptions such as that London could have 40, there could be 9 in York and 3 in Lincoln. If such laws had ever come near to succeeding, there would be nothing like the 82,000 licensed premises of today nor the wonderful proliferation of signs.

Perhaps the greatest influence on the development of the modern pub sign was the illiteracy of the majority of people until late in the nineteenth century. This was the direct cause of signs being pictorial in the first place as well as the pictures being large, bright and relatively simple and straightforward. Animals, being so familiar, were very popular sign subjects in addition to the previously mentioned religious symbols and heraldic devices. Even animals could cause confusion, though. A pub in Colnbrook, believed to be one of the oldest in England, is named the Ostrich. This was actually an heraldic pun on the word hospice (To honour a nearby hospice). But the locals had never seen an Ostrich so the pub was commonly called the Crane!

Some other easily recognizable and understandable early signs were the Sun, the Ship and pictorials showing symbols of various trades such as the Horseshoes and the Hammer and Nails.

Queen Elizabeth I had a strong and direct influence on pubs and pub signs. The Queen travelled throughout the realm more widely than earlier monarchs and was said to be unhappy about the state of the inns for travellers like herself. She urged that many new inns be built. So, today, the traveller will see many obviously old pubs named the New Inn.

This was not, however, the only source of that name. The other, simpler beginning was when a second pub or inn was built in a community. Naturally, it would be called 'the new inn'.

Queen Elizabeth was also very angry with the way she was depicted on pub signs. She didn't mind being on the signs, but objected to the poor likenesses. So she issued one approved painting which had to be copied faithfully. The other versions 'by unskillful and common painters should be knocked to pieces and cast into the fire'. In more modern times, royalty has taken another approach. Queen Victoria (perhaps for reasons similar to Queen Elizabeth) decreed that no pub sign or advertising material could show a living member of royalty. The Lord Chamberlain is charged with enforcing this ban. He recently had to exercise his powers. When the Prince of Wales married, a number of pub signs showed the new Princess of Wales and had to be changed. Occasionally pub sign artists will either boldly or subtly show a royal on a sign just to see if they can 'get away with it'. They don't!

Legislation continued to follow pubs and pub signs throughout the centuries. In the first year of the reign of King James I, an act defined 'the ancient, true and principal use of inns, ale-houses and victualling houses' as being for 'the resort, relief and lodging of wayfaring people, travelling from place to place'. The common denominator was still that beer was brewed on the premises for sale and consumption there. That distinction would continue until the eighteenth century when the growth of the separate and, later, mighty brewers began.

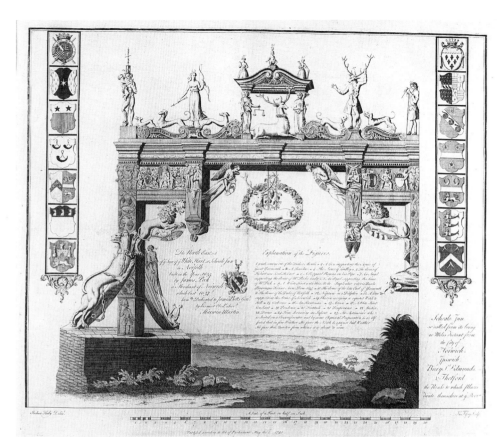

The White Hart, Scoale. This sign in Lincolnshire was the most dramatic and ostentatious ever erected. The print on the facing page shows this vast sign in its context.

In 1648 a shortage of small coins and precious metals in Britain brought about an interesting situation for pubs and an equally interesting sidelight to the story of pub signs. Because of the lack of coins, it was considered legal for pubs and other trades to make and issue tokens. These were in the values of farthings, halfpennies and pennies. They were redeemable for money or goods in the issuing pub or shop and became common currency in the areas around the issuing establishment. Pubs normally put the publican's name and a promise to pay on one side and the pub sign and name on the reverse. The coins were cheaply made of copper or brass and this is the origin of the phrase 'a brass farthing'. These tokens were in common and legal use until about 1672. Until the early 1800s pub tokens were still in evidence but their use was usually restricted to the pub itself. For example, pubs which had some entertainment as part of a day's programme would charge an admission fee and give the patron a token or two which would be used for food or drink.

Pubs were becoming ever more competitive and one of the chief ways to attract customers was with a notable pub sign. Signs were being made constantly bigger and more elaborate. In 1655 the largest pub sign ever built

In the seventeenth century, there was a serious shortage of precious metal for the minting of official coins. So publicans and other tradesmen were allowed to make and issue trade tokens legally during a 20 year period. These were normally about the size of a modern 1p coin although thinner and were stamped in brass or copper. The tokens were in values of farthings, halfpennies and pennies and the phrase 'a brass farthing' dates from this time. Pubs issued the tokens to be used for food or drink at the pub and promised to redeem them for official money. The tokens came to be used in the areas around the issuing tradesman and were generally accepted as money. The tokens showed the publican's name and promise to pay on one side while the other side would show the pub sign and its name and location.

This picture shows two seventeenth-century tokens at the top. One is a halfpenny issued by Samuel Wood at the Saracen's Head in Ashford, Kent in 1666. The other is a halfpenny by Jeremiah Masterson at Chequers in Canterbury.

The other four tokens are from a much later period, probably the early 1800s. While not acceptable as legal coins, they were used by pubs as promotional devices and as part of a package. That is, pubs with entertainment or dancing would charge an overall admission and give the guest one or more tokens to be used for food and drink during the evening. These four are from the Tun, The Swan with Two Necks, the Star and the Greyhound, all in London.

was erected by James Peck at the White Hart in Scoale at a cost of over £1000! The sign stretched over the highway and was thus described by Sir Thomas Browne in 1663, 'I came to Scoale where there is a very handsome inn and the noblest signpost in England about and upon which was carved a great many stories as of Charon and Cerberus, Actaeon and Diana and many others; the sign itself is a White Hart, which hangs down carved in a stately wreath'. The stately wreath, of course, looking a lot like an ale-garland.

Then, and perhaps because of the White Hart, in 1667 an act decreed that there could be no more signs stretching across the roadway (so-called Gallows signs) but must be hung from a balcony or from the side of the house. A few gallows signs remain. The Four Swans at Waltham Cross, Herts. cannot be removed without an act of Parliament. There is the Green Man and Black's Head at Ashbourne, Derbyshire and the Olde Starre in York. Early in the eighteenth century an oversized and overweight sign in London's Fleet Street fell and dragged down the front wall of the pub with it, killing two young ladies, the king's jeweller and a cobbler. That and other abuses led to even more regulations until today the vast majority of signs are roughly uniform in size. Most today measure about four feet by three feet.

The next major development to affect pubs and pub signs happened during the eighteenth and nineteenth centuries. At that time over 1000 miles of roads were built throughout Britain which led to the development of the coaching inns, wonderfully picturesque with courtyards and galleries and the romantic notions of coaches and highwaymen. But the era was short lived because the steam train became a reality in 1825. To meet the demands of the new kind of travellers as well as the railway station staff itself, new pubs were established near the stations. Many of these had accommodation and, in fact, many called themselves hotels. A lot of the old coaching inns and railway hotels have changed their names as transportation again changed in

The Four Swans, Waltham Cross, Hertfordshire, from a watercolour dating from the early nineteenth century.

nature. Sadly, because they were interesting architecturally as well as being good pubs, many closed when their trade dropped off. Next came the Victorian era with its overdone, beautiful and elaborate, curved, cut and stained glass and polished wood in city and town centres. Fortunately, many of these are still flourishing.

That briefly, is the history, legend and tradition that shaped the pubs and pub signs we see today. Except where it will be mentioned as part of the background of a particular sign, enough of history. Because this is a book to celebrate the art of the pub sign and, for the most part, that means a living, popular art of today. There will be some signs from the past but those, like this chapter, are to set the stage for the art that is around us now.

The Four Swans, Waltham
Cross, in more recent times. One
of the finest surviving 'gallows'
signs.

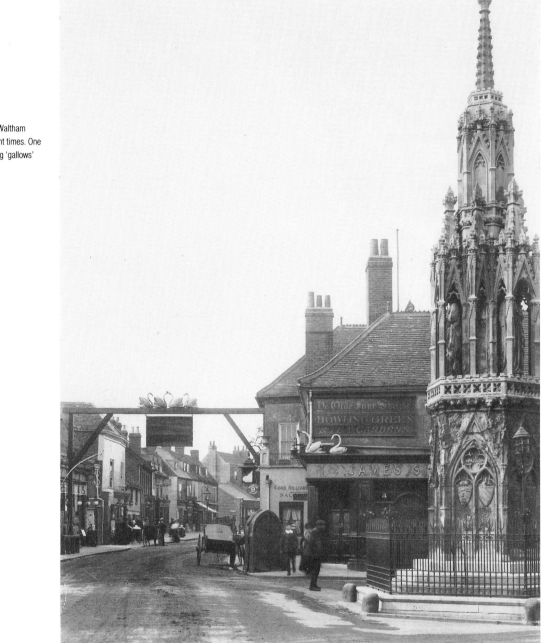

One side of **The Green Man and Black's Head** at Ashbourne in Derbyshire. It has both a traditional painted sign and a 'gallows' over the road.

An elaborate metal bracket for a pub sign at **The Bell**, Stilton.

The other side of **The Green Man and Black's Head**, Ashbourne.

The marvellous **Three Swans** sign in Melton Mowbray, its refined metalwork is a rare eighteenth-century survival.

Chapter 2

THE PUB SIGN IN LONDON

'On Saturday next before the Feast of our Lord's Nativity, in the 10th year etc., Thomas Stokes was brought before the Mayor and Aldermen and questioned for that he had pretended to be an officer and a taker of ale for the household of our said Lord the King; and under such colour, at divers times within the preceding eight days, had gone to the houses of several brewers, namely, John at Cok on the Hop, adjoining the Brethren of the Holy Cross, near to the Tower of London, William Roke at Graschirche, John atte Blakeloft in the Vintry, in London, and divers other houses in the same city, and there marked several barrels full of ale with a mark, called 'arewehede,' saying that those barrels were for the household of our Lord the King; whereas in truth he was not then any officer belonging to the same our Lord the King; and thus falsely and deceitfully he received divers sums of money from the brewers aforesaid, that he might have their ale in peace; to the scandal of our said Lord the King, and all his officers, and in manifest deceit of the people.'

The above account, written in 1386, gives a vivid picture of ale-production in fourteenth-century London and of the brewers, their ecclesiastical links and the consumers, ranging from the royal household to

The brewers Watney Mann kept a unique photographic record of their pubs in and around London during the late nineteenth-century. Many of their houses were photographed on or before the day they opened, presenting us with a chance to see Victorian pubs in pristine condition. On the following pages are a number which typify the appearance of London pubs at that time. This page shows **The Giraffe**, Penton Place, Wallworth, London; opposite is the **White Horse**, Woolwich Road, London.

the artful Thomas Stokes. The sign of the Cock on the Hoop was most likely an adaptation of the Hoop and Grapes which is considered to be one of the earliest pictorial tavern signs and there are many examples to be found in early records, the 'Mayden en la Hope' (1350), the 'Swanne on the Hoope' (1414), the 'Belle on the Hope' (1387) and 'Le Kay sur le Hoope' (1391).

The Hoop and Grapes is certainly an old name, and the pub of that name in Aldgate High Street claims to be one of the oldest surviving licensed houses in London. The Hoop and Grapes at 80 Farringdon Street on the other hand used to be known as Nash's, and was renamed because in 1921 the publican discovered in his attic a very old sign depicting a bunch of grapes, 'whereupon he caused it to be suspended with a new iron hoop from the bracket of the pre-war outside lamp'. Unfortunately it disappeared soon after and was replaced by a lettered sign.

In 1309 there were 354 taverns and 1334 brew-houses in London. Up until the end of the fifteenth century signs were of basic construction but gradually as competition increased they became more elaborate. 'The very signs at their doors are gorgeous, costing £30 or £40 perhaps,' wrote William Harrison in his *Description of England* in 1577.

The majority of Watney Mann pubs did not have a pub sign as we understand it. These however are exceptions – **The Ship**, Croydon High Street; **The Mother Shipton**, Malden Road, Camden, and **The Gun**, Lupus Street, London.

More frequently the name of the pub was expressed by a carved plaque or statue. Clockwise from top left – **The Bull's Head**, York Street, Westminster; **The Three Goats Heads**, Wandsworth Road, Lambeth; **The Black Bull**, Holborn; **The Lion**, Holford Street, Mile End; **The King's Head**, Mile End; **The Prince of Wales**, Drury Lane.

Occasionally, a London pub would display its name, not on a sign or on a sculptured freize, but engraved upon its lamp. This is **The Feathers**, Great Smith Street,

The Spotted Dog, Willesden, London. A good example of a Victorian typographical sign.

The Unwin Arms, Haringay Grove.

Some 19th-century London pubs exhibited no depiction of their name at all. One wonders what modern pub sign artists would make of **The Monster**, Pimlico, and **The Pineapple**, Graham Street.

A seventeenth-century view of Cheapside, London, showing **The Nag's Head**.

Horses have always been depicted on signs in London. In 1356 the sign of the Horse's Head in the parish of St Vedast is mentioned, whilst Le Serre's print showing the procession of Mary of Medici of 1638 depicts the sign of the Nag's Head in Cheapside. Suspended at the end of the protruding post is an ale-garland which traditionally advertised a new brew.

A Nag's Head in Whitechapel Road existed in 1661 and on the other side of the road the Horse and Leaping Bar could be found, named after a neighbouring horse-training ground. The sign of the Nag's Head in Floral Street, Covent Garden, depicts a circus horse due to the pub's theatrical associations.

In the eighteenth century, stables were to be found behind elegant town houses in fashionable areas like Belgravia and the Horse and Groom pub sign originates from this time. Several examples can still be found in central London as the name has continued to be very popular.

The White Horse, Fetter Lane was a busy coaching inn, dating from the seventeenth century and was demolished in 1899. An old engraving shows the name of the inn in bold lettering across the facade with a model of a white horse raised above it.

A similar use of a three-dimensional sign could be found at the Cock Inn, Leadenhall Street, which existed until the early 1800s. The sign of the 'Cock and Bottle' has a long history and an inn of that name could be found in Cannon Street. The original tiled sign from about 1700 is now in the Museum of London. The Cock in Fleet Street was formerly known as the Cock and Bottle and was situated on the opposite side of the road. The sign is all that remains of the original pub, Grinling Gibbons is said to have carved it in the seventeenth century, though this is not proven. Samuel Pepys visited the tavern with Mrs Knipp, the attractive actress, as did Thackeray, Tennyson and Dickens.

The history of several other London inn signs depicting birds is also of

The coach for Cambridge leaving
The White Horse, Fetter Lane.

A seventeenth-century tiled sign
for **The Cock and Bottle**, now in
the Museum of London.

The Cock, Leadenhall Street.

The Tabard in the seventeenth-century.

interest as they often indicate a corruption of a name. The Swan with Two Necks, which was in Lad Lane, was a busy nineteenth-century coaching terminus, its name being a corruption of the Swan with Two Nicks which referred to the markings made on swans' bills as a mark of ownership.

Another example of a general misinterpretation of a pub sign which became permanent is the Goose and Gridiron. The inn had been called the Mitre until it was burnt down in the Great Fire. When it was rebuilt, its name was changed to the Lyre and Swan, the emblem of the Society of Musicians which met there. The swan and its complicated heraldry failed to be understood and it became popularly known as the Goose and Gridiron. The name was changed officially when the pub was rebuilt at a later date. E. A. Schalch adds a further interesting note to this well known story, 'English sailors used to call the Eagle and Stripes, which was the design of the American flag before the Stars took the place of the Eagle and Stripes, by the same nickname.'

In 1976 the Poppinjay was opened in Fleet Street. Although a modern pub, its sign refers to a medieval custom. The Poppinjay is located on the site where the Abbots of Cirencester resided and who used the sign of this particular bird as their emblem. Each May the Festival of the Poppinjay took place; replicas of the bird were placed on poles and used as a target by archers.

In 1598 Stow wrote in his survey, 'towards London Bridge on the same side, be many fair inns for the receipt; by these signs: the Spurre, Christopher, Bull, Queen's Head, Tabard, George, Hart, King's Head.'

The Tabard, Borough High Street, originated in the early fourteenth century. It was a popular wayside tavern made famous by Geoffrey Chaucer in his *Canterbury Tales* which he began in 1373. A seventeenth-century print shows the Tabard at this time, a traditional 'gallows' structure with a

The Tabard Inn, Southwark, in
the early nineteenth century.

The King's Head Tavern shown,
left, in a view of Fenchurch Street
in the 1750s.

pictorial sign hanging from it indicates the establishment in no uncertain terms. Another print of 1810 shows the sign suspended from the gallery, no doubt a result of the legislation in 1797 ordering the 'taking down of all signs which projected or which in any way could be considered an encroachment or annoyance.'

Stow says that the name of the Tabard derives from the, 'Jacquit, or sleevelesse coat, whole before, open on both sides, with a square coller, winged at the shoulders,' which was worn by heralds. In the late seventeenth century this name was changed to the Talbot, a breed of dog with a turned up tail but later in the eighteenth century, the pub once again became known as the Tabard.

Royal names and heraldic sources have long been a popular choice as a pub sign in London. There are references to the sign of the King's Head at Bow (1662), Chancery Lane (1472), Exchange Alley (1663) and New Fish Street (1417) and there are eleven pubs using the name in central London today. The King's Head tavern in Fenchurch Street, shown in a print of 1751, was later known as the London Tavern and was destroyed in 1941. The print indicates how distinctive a good pub sign could be in the days when it did not have to compete with advertising material such as posters and hoardings which covered every possible surface by the nineteenth century.

The sign of the King's Head in Chiswell Street commemorates a visit in 1787 by George III and Queen Charlotte to the adjoining Whitbread Brewery in order to view Samuel Whitbread's latest innovations in ale-production.

Queen Elizabeth I's disapproval of the manner in which she was depicted on inn signs has already been mentioned but in the eighteenth century her portrait adorned the sign of the Queen's Head and Artichoke in Albany Street. It was said that one of the royal gardeners had built the house and in 1885 the sign of this pub was described by John Thomas Smith in his charmingly titled *A Book for a Rainy Day*: 'it was much weather beaten, though perhaps once a tolerably good portrait of Queen Elizabeth.'

Queen Anne's portrait can be seen at the sign of the Queen, Wandsworth. Her early years were spent at Wandsworth Manor House. She is also connected with the famous Dolly's Chop House near St Paul's Cathedral. This was originally called the Queen's Head, the sign being a painting of the last Stuart sovereign. The new vivacious hostess, however, became very popular and Gainsborough's portrait of Dolly replaced that of Queen Anne. The pub was pulled down in 1883.

Foreign royalty is represented by the Empress of Russia in E.C.1 and the King of Bohemia in Hampstead. In 1698 Peter the Great visited Holland to study shipbuilding, he worked alongside the ordinary men and eventually arrived in England where he continued his 'apprenticeship'. It is said that the Czar could consume vast quantities of alcohol and the landlord of his favourite pub commemorated his stay by having the Czar's portrait painted and hung up as a sign. The original was replaced in 1808.

Just as Edward III had ordered the ale-stakes of taverns to be reduced in length in 1375, so an act was passed during the reign of Charles II after the Great Fire of London in 1666, forbidding the use of hanging signs. New establishments often resorted to signs carved in stone which were placed on the exterior walls. The sign of the Bell is one example. It now forms part of

The sign of **The Bell** from Knightrider Street, London.

The Bull and Mouth, St Martins-le-Grand, London.

the Museum of London collection but used to serve a pub in Knightrider Street. A similar sign is that of the former Bull and Mouth in St Martin's le Grand which was an important early nineteenth-century coaching inn serving the North-West of England. There is a pub of the same name in Bloomsbury Way. The origin of the sign stems from a corruption of 'Boulogne Mouth'. The sign of the Bull and Gate is also said to be derived in this manner relating to Henry VIII's removal of the gates of Boulogne when he captured the city in 1544.

The Mother Redcap Holloway had a painted sign showing a robin feeding her young, but the original sign was far more eye catching. A rather menacing old lady was accompanied by the rhyme:

Old Mother Red Cap, according to her tale,
Lived twenty and a hundred years by drinking this good ale.
It was her meat, it was her drink, and medicine beside,
And if she still had drunk good ale, she never would have died.

Pepys describes it in his Diary on 24 September 1661, 'So we rode easily through and only drinking at Halloway at the sign of a woman with Cakes in one hand and a pot of ale in the other, which did give good occasions of mirth, resembling her to the mayd that served us; we got home very timely and well. It is said that Moll Cutpurse the highwaywoman frequented this pub during the English Civil War.'

The Blue Posts is another popular London pub sign. The name derives from the times when signs were positioned on two posts, and the latter came to represent a pub as much as the sign itself. One example is the Blue Posts in Bennett Street which was named after the posts which stood in the old courtyard. During the seventeenth century, blue Sedan chairs could be hired from this establishment and the name could also derive from this source.

In London, as elsewhere, one finds a number of 'Angels'. The Angel at Bishopsgate Street is where the Parish Clerks of London were based in the thirteenth century. Another, the Angel in Rotherhithe Street, was originally named the Salutation but this was felt to be too resonent of Catholicism and was changed after the Reformation. Pepys who admired pubs visited this one, and alledgedly bought cherries for his wife here. He was also familiar with pubs of the same name in King Street and Tower Hill. Popham gives us further information on the use of the Angel: 'Until well into the seventeenth century we see signboards depicting the angel holding a scroll on which the words are invariably 'Ave Maria, gratia plena, Dominus tecum.''

The most famous Angel, in Islington, was well known to all Londoners until it was demolished in 1819. Many travellers would spend the night safely at this inn rather than run the risk of encountering outlaws on the dark route into the city. London as the capital of a rising industrial power and as the heart of the British Empire, continually added to its number of pubs; especially in the nineteenth century.

By 1843 London could boast 4400 public houses, 330 hotels and 960 wine and spirit shops. As more and more people were learning to read there was less need for painted or three-dimensional emblematic pub signs; instead, the names of pubs were painted in prominent lettering across the façade. Pub signs as such began to decline in popularity, and the advent of a new commercial era, in which beer was no longer brewed on the premises but supplied by a public brewery, was marked by the appearance of the

The Two Brewers, Tottenham.

The Bolt in Tun and the detail of its signboard, formerly of Fleet Street.

company's advertising board, e.g. the Two Brewers Tottenham. The decline in traditional pub signs was, in some instances, mitigated by excellent examples of signwriting which in its own way proved to be a decorative addition to London pubs. A print of the Bolt in Tun in Fleet Street in 1859, for example, shows the combined use of the traditional signs together with contemporary signwriting.

The City of Salisbury, Tooley Street, was built in 1888 and retained one link with the history of long established pub decoration: this was the chequer board frieze beneath the windows. Draughts and chess had always been popular pub games and the distinctive board was frequently used as the sign of an inn. The chequered design to be found on coats of arms has also been sited as a possible origin and the sign was also used by moneychangers. Inspite of this the present day pub the Chequers in Duke Street now displays a painting of the prime minister's country residence of the same name.

Despite the declining need for carved signs or representative sculptures many London pubs during the nineteenth century displayed novel ideas in this field, often placed high up on the pediment. The Jolly Gardeners at Lambeth had a delicately carved stone panel illustrating two gardeners looking more whimsical than jolly whilst the Yorkshire Grey in the Gray's Inn Road was topped by a soldier complete with horse, sword and castle. The Pakenham Knightsbridge Green had a frieze of vines and other typical motifs above the upper windows, crowned by two graceful racehorses in low relief.

The famous Elephant and Castle was demolished in 1961 and its sign was placed on display in the new shopping precinct. The pub of the same name at Vauxhall Bridge still has its elephant in situ. Popham doubts whether the name originated as a corruption of the 'Infanta of Castille' who became consort to Edward I and suggests that a feasible derivation is from the emblem of the Cutler's Company and their links with the ivory trade. Nonetheless the 'castle' certainly refers to the howdah on the elephant's back.

The introduction of gaslights outside pubs during the early nineteenth

The City of Salisbury, Tooley Street, London, built in 1888.

A carved relief for **The Jolly Gardeners**, Black Prince Road, Lambeth, of 1890.

A Yorkshire Grey carved by 'Mr Plows' at the **Yorkshire Grey**, Grays Inn Road.

The Pakenham, Knightsbridge Green.

The Elephant and Castle, Vauxhall.

The New Jolly Caulkers in
Rotherhythe, by Cosmo Clark.

The Old Spotted Dog, Neasden.

An eighteenth-century engraving
by Cruikshank showing pub signs
used in a political context, to
satirical effect.

century contributed to the decline of the painted sign. The glowing lamps suspended from brackets on the exterior proved highly successful in attracting those passing by. Frequently the name of the pub was painted on the lamps themselves, being clearly visible during the day and particularly so in the evening once illuminated. 'As the street lights dimly lit up in the twilight the pubs lit up far more brightly; long rows of monstrous lanterns stretched out into the street on curling and caparisoned tentacles of wrought iron and underneath them walls of sinuously bending and elaborately engraved glass were lit from the inside by an inner row of blazing globes.' The continued mechanization of what had been crafts affected the decoration of pubs. The increased availability of engraved glass, for example, encouraged its use in a number of ornate designs. A pub's name offered an obvious example, although it usually became strictly an exercise in the engravers' calligraphic skills, rather than a pictorial representation. The combined attractions of sparkling glass and gaslight were considered far superior to the traditional painted sign board, and only perhaps the power of typically British nostalgia brought them back into vogue in the twentieth century.

It was during the 1930s that a marked revival of painted pub signs developed. In September 1932 *The Times* actively encouraged this trend by featuring several articles on the subject: 'On the face of it a pleasant inn sign means a pleasant inn beneath it. But an inn sign which is nothing but an advertisement for beer is open to the interpretation that the inn is only a beer-house, and that no trouble will be taken over any visitors who may want anything more than beer.'

The culmination of this new interest was the Inn Signs Exhibition held at the Building Centre, in Bond Street, in November 1936, which attracted 18,000 visitors. The sign of the Old Spotted Dog in Neasden Lane painted by Ralph Ellis is representative of the emphasis on simplicity and good design which typifies pub signs of this period. The sign for the New Jolly Caulkers in Rotherhithe designed and painted by Mr Cosmo Clark is unusual in that it was executed on glass. It graphically displays three caulkers driving plate-joins together on a ship's deck.

After the Second World War the fabric of London went through dramatic changes in the hands of planners and developers. Although large parts of London were demolished, traditional pubs survived and while over-shadowed by new high-rise office blocks continued to provide an important service. Passing crazes for more sophisticated forms of entertainment, the fashion for theme pubs and wine bars, failed to usurp the position of the London pub.

The interest in conservation and Britain's heritage which developed during the 1970s encouraged another revival of interest not only in the social role of public houses but also their decoration and signs. Added to this was the increasingly important role of tourism and the pubs of London remain hugely popular with visitors from far and wide.

The corporate identities of the large breweries, the use of neon signs and other unsuitable effects have had a damaging influence but pub signs remain and London would not be the same place without them. Certainly no one wandering around the capital would relish their disappearance, and London is a splendid 'gallery' of pub sign art.

Chapter 3

PUB SIGN ARTISTS OF THE PAST

If you see a pub sign you particularly like, photograph it, talk to the publican about it, ask if he or the brewery can tell you more about the artist and where he has other signs hung, but do it *now*! The weather, traffic, vandalism or some other natural or unnatural cause will get to it and it will be gone forever. At best a pub sign will last about ten years and by then the publican may have been changed, the artist may have died or moved on to other things, the brewery may decide on a different interpretation of the pub name and even if the image is to be repeated, a less talented artist may do so.

This art form is, sadly, transient. Paintings created with every bit as much talent and care as any that hang in museums and galleries will be gone in a blink of history's eye. Further compounding the short life of a sign in place on a pub is what happens to it when it is taken down. That mostly depends on the board it is painted on and the condition of that board. If it is sound, whether it be wood or metal, the paint will be stripped off, the board reprimed and a new painting painted on it. Occasionally a new painting will just be painted on top of the old. Worn and not re-usable boards are simply discarded. There are a few collectors of old pub signs (the author being one) who go around to artists and signwriters seeking old boards. These collectors are few because of the condition of most old boards, their size and weight and the difficulty of displaying and enjoying such large paintings.

In the past this situation was much worse. Since the very beginning, pub signs were primarily and rightly considered to be a commercial attention getter. Only very rarely was any thought given to preserving the paintings. In a few cases, the publican or brewer liked a painting or believed the artist was good and going on to greater fame and so saved his work. Or, accidentally, old boards were kept in a barn or shed or cellar simply because no one thought to throw them out.

Because of this, our knowledge of great artists of the past who painted pub signs is very limited. Logic tells us that probably most artists painted signs. Early in the artist's career and before he is well known and busy, he will typically turn his hand to anything which will show off his talent and put some food on the table. And where better to look for food (and drink!) than the local pub. Richard Wilson (1714–1782), the classical landscape painter of the eighteenth century and George Morland (1763–1804) were both known to paint pub signs for their bread and butter. Morland was especially known to paint a sign for the price of a meal and once for 'unlimited gin'. He painted sentimental genre and rural life scenes. His father Henry Robert Morland was a painter, restorer and dealer to whom George was apprenticed for 7 years from 1777: his tasks included copying and forging Dutch landscapes. He exhibited at the Royal Academy from 1781 to 1804, and to 1778 his characteristic works were small sentimental genre scenes, followed in the 1790s by larger pictures of rustic scenes, wreckers and smugglers. In later years, he produced a very large number of what we would call 'pot-boilers'. His work was very much copied and faked. In later life he was frequently drunk, and when not in prison, busily trying to avoid his creditors.

Richard Wilson (1714–1782) trained as a portraitist in London and had his own practice by 1744, although he also experimented in topographical painting before a Venice trip in 1750. In Rome by 1752, he then turned to landscape, influenced by the Roman Campagna and the works of Claude and Poussin, the result was his own type of classical landscape. He was a founder

George Morland painted pub signs for food, and on one occasion for 'draughts of gin!' No original sign that he painted is known to survive, but this genre scene, dated 1792 and entitled 'The Public House Door' does show a subject unusually close, one supposes, to his heart.

member of the Society of Artists and then the Royal Academy, exhibiting from 1769 to 1780, producing italianized Welsh scenes and enjoying some success as a 'country house' portraitist. By the 1770s, however, the more picturesque landscapes of Zuccarelli were preferred to Wilson's classically inspired scenes. He was given the sinecure of RA Librarianship and died in impoverished circumstances.

In addition to Morland and Wilson, some founders and early members of the Royal Academy were sign painters. Samuel Wale (1721–1786) was born in London and apprenticed to a silver plate engraver. He studied drawing at St Martin's Lane Academy and painted ceiling pieces but his main employment was as a book illustrator. It's claimed that he 'painted some signs and one of "Shakespeare" was of some notoriety'. After Wilson's death Wale was appointed RA Librarian. He exhibited at the Academy from 1769 to 1778 (usually historical scenes) and works by him are in Bethlem, Christ, St Thomas and Foundling Hospitals. He produced illustrations for *London and its Environs Described* (1761) and for an edition of Isaak Walton's *Angler*. Edward Penny (1714–1791) was a painter of portraits, histories and moral subjects. He studied with Thomas Hudson (1701–1779) and Benefial in Rome and returned to England in 1743, first practising in his native Cheshire and then in London, specializing in small-scale full lengths, similar to Zoffany's work later, and was listed as 'eminent painter' in the *Universal Magazine*. He exhibited at the Society of Artists from 1762 to 1768 and was Vice President in 1765. Work shows an interest in works of charity and was very popular as engravings. He gave up painting in 1782 and according to Redgrave, married well. Also according to Redgrave he designed illustrations for an edition of *The Novelists*.

Eighteenth-Century Sketches

In 1984, Sotheby's auctioned the impressive art collection of the late Lord Clark of Saltwood including, surprisingly, an album of designs for pub signs. The album contains 84 pages, each with a bold design in watercolours mixed with oil. It is believed to be the sketch book of a journeyman artist, one he would show to prospective clients to get approval for the pub sign he would paint – just as today's artists often submit sketches to their brewery clients. The paper was watermarked with a Strasbourg Lily and is generally associated with the late 1750s and early 1760s. The identity of the artist is unknown but one sketch was signed J. Wooton. The album was expected to bring between £4000 and £6000 but was sold for £28,000. Since it is almost impossible to see pub signs from over 200 years ago, this album gives a rare chance to see that pub signs in the 1700s looked very much like those of today.

Jimmy Young was a publican but for many years now has been a writer, mapmaker and historian. He is holding his most prized pub sign. It is The College Kitchen from Cathedral Close in Exeter and dates from the 1830s. Jimmy believes it was hung in a sort of protected vestibule which would protect it from the worst of the weather and that is why, despite years of smoke and dirt, it is in comparatively good condition today.

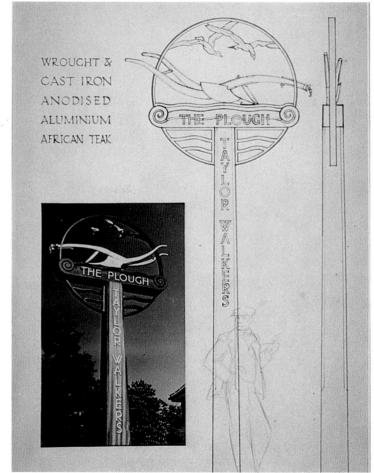

A Man Loaded With Mischief Is this the original William Hogarth painting of this most famous pub sign? Or was the one shown in the 1907 *Illustrated London News* the real Hogarth? Are they both copies? No one really knows. Books on pub sign history agree that the sign was taken down and preserved but disagree as to what happened to it. The references are vague, saying it was owned by a woman in St. Albans or by an unnamed brewery. This photograph could well show the original. It is hanging in Grand Metropolitan Brewing's Brick Lane brewery in London. The present day staff cannot say categorically that it is the original Hogarth but the brewery did acquire it from a politician in St. Albans.

The sculptor F Ayres was perhaps best known for his work at the BBC, but like a number of other artists, turned his talents to pub sign design. This is a delicate original sketch for his monumental metal sign for The Plough, Brent, together with a photograph of the finished work.

The Boscobel Oak, the sign for The Royal Oak Inn at Bettys-y-Coed, painted by David Cox in 1847, and much admired since.

A portrait of the 'Elder' Crome of Norwich.

David Cox (1783–1859), was a watercolourist. His early years were spent as a scene painter in Birmingham and London and he became known for his rural anecdotal scenes which were very popular in the late nineteenth century. From c. 1844, he made annual sketching trips to Wales and based himself in Bettws-y-Coed at the Royal Oak. In 1847 he painted a sign, in oil, representing Charles II in the oak tree at Boscobel, and also painted a fresco in the pub parlour. The painting was moved inside and placed under glass by the landlady. In 1880, when she was retiring, she attempted to take it with her as being her private property. The brewery disagreed and took her to court. The court decided in favour of the brewery and the painting was kept at the pub.

John Berney Crome (1768–1821) known as 'Old' Crome was born in Norwich. His father was a journeyman weaver who also kept an ale-house called the Griffen, then in Conisford, now King Street, Norwich. At fifteen he was apprenticed to Francis Whisler, a coach and sign-painter, working as the latter until, presumably, 1798 when he is recorded as drawing master at Earlham Hall. According to his patron, Dawson Turner, Crome entered into a form of commercial art partnership (pre-1798) with Robert Ladrooke, producing inn signs, decorating cakes and copying prints. 'Old' Crome painted a sign for the Jolly Sailor at Yarmouth. The sign was later sold at an auction in Norwich for twelve guineas in 1906. Crome's pub sign may still exist. The Victoria and Albert Museum in London has a pub sign painted by Old Crome which is called 'The Wherryman' but might well be called 'The Jolly Sailor' by a viewer not knowing its correct title. C. R. Leslie (1774–1859) and J. E. Hodgson (1831–1895) each took a side of the sign of the George and Dragon at Wargrave-on-Thames in 1874. This was said to have been done to settle their bill. Leslie's painting depicted the saint in combat with the dragon and Hodgson's painting showed the slain dragon and St George drinking from a tankard.

Other nineteenth-century artists were involved in pub signs in one way or another. Sir John Everett Millais (1829–96), began as an eleven-year-old prodigy of RA Schools, and was a founder member of the Pre-Raphaelite Brotherhood, with Holman Hunt and Rossetti in 1848. In the 1820s he contributed comic drawings for *Punch* but on the condition that his name was not printed. Later works were portraits, and he became very wealthy. In his youth, he painted a George and Dragon, at Hayes Common in Middlesex. Walter Crane (1808–1809) painted a sign for the Fox & Pelican at Graysholt, Hampshire. Sir William Charles Ross (1794–1860) was apprenticed to a miniature-painter but soon established his own reputation. Queen Victoria's commission led to others from Albert and from a number of European Royal

Portraits of Sir John Millais, Sir William Ross and William Hogarth.

Families. He produced over 2000 miniatures on ivory. In his young days, he is said to have painted a sign for the Magpie at Sudbury. The landlady proudly said that thirty years later, Sir Charles visited the inn and asked to see the sign once more.

William Hogarth (1697–1764) is, of course, the best known of the artists associated with pub signs. His sign of the 'Man Loaded with Mischief' was once to be seen in Oxford Street. It reportedly still exists, being in a brewery or in private hands in St Albans. Certainly many copies and imitations of the painting still exist. The sign showed a man carrying on his shoulders, fastened by the chains of wedlock, a drunken wife with a raven and a monkey. The sign was painted in great detail with Hogarth's usual keen and caustic wit. Pub signs also appeared in many of his other works, usually to add to the satire or strengthen a point. In his famous engraving Gin Lane, all the signs are of death and debt; while in Beer St., the signs are happy and welcoming and the sign-painter, shown at his work, is happy and satisfied with himself.

In the middle of the eighteenth century, Harp Alley, Shoe Lane was the centre of the sign-painters in London and was certainly known by Hogarth. In 1762 a well known wag named Bonnell Thornton organized an Exhibition of Signboards in order to make fun of the exhibitions of the Society of Artists. The exhibition, which was supposedly sponsored by the nonexistent Society of Sign-painters, was a huge success with the public. But there were

William Hogarth's 'Beer Street', 1751.

William Hogarth's 'Gin Lane', 1751.

William Hogarth's famous 'Beer Street' boldly declares that beer was as good for individuals and England as gin was shown to be bad in his 'Gin Lane'. All of the people on Beer Street are healthy, happily enjoying their pints while building and prosperity abound.

As usual with Hogarth, there is a wealth of humourous detail. The only person not doing well is the pawnbroker; his door is shut tight and his sign is sagging but even he is being given a pint by a boy.

Hogarth's affection for pub sign painters is obvious in the contented, happy expression on the face of the artist in this picture. Perhaps he was thinking of his own feelings when he painted a pub sign. There are three pub signs visible. The pub in the background has the sign of a brightly shining sun, again reflecting good cheer and happiness. On the corner of The Sun, a chequerboard is painted

on the wall. The same chequered pattern is on the pole the painter is adorning. Since Roman days, this meant that games, particularly chess, are played in that pub. It evolved into a pub sign frequently seen today, The Chequers. Chequers also gained popularity as a pub sign because it was part of the arms of the Earls of Warrene in the Middle Ages who had the responsibility for licensing and regulating pubs. Then there is a small sign, directly below the pictorial Hogarth's artist is painting. It shows a loaf of bread and a jug with beer flowing into a goblet. This indicates the food and drink available in the pub.

The sign being painted is the Health to the Barley Mow, showing people dancing on and around a barley mow, mugs in hand. The Barley Mow and the Health to the Barley Mow were popular signs, mostly appearing in the countryside. They reflected the joy of the farmers on having a good crop. Once again, Hogarth is saying that beer is related to good cheer, a successful crop and health.

The Crown Another special item in the Luton Museum collection is The Crown, a pub sign from The Crown in Northill. This crown was made by a blacksmith in the eighteenth century.

Plume of Feathers This symbol

is still used as a popular pub sign, but with varying names. It is sometimes the Prince of Wales, the Prince's Feathers, the Feathers and the Feathers Royal among other variations. All refer to the plume of three ostrich feathers which became the crest of the Black Prince. In this case, the Plume of Feathers was painted for a pub in Luton. The pub was then owned, early in this century, by J.W. Green brewery. This sign, which is in quite good condition, is part of the Luton Museum collection.

many angry and sarcastic articles in the daily papers. Each time one of these was written, the 'Society' would respond by thanking the critic for his thoughts and for publicizing the exhibition. Hogarth gleefully joined in and included several works under the obvious false name of Hogarty. He also was a member of the 'hanging committee' and reportedly used his pencil to change some details in others' works. In companion portraits of the Empress Maria Theresa and the King of Prussia, he changed the cast of their eyes so that they appeared to leer at each other. His 'A Man Loaded with Mischief' was included in the show but this could have been a second version of the pub sign – perhaps explaining the confusion as to whether this sign still exists and where it is. Hogarth probably had a hand in two exhibits which caused great talk. Each was hidden behind a blue curtain (the signal at that time that the art behind the curtains might give offence to the delicate). Behind the first, 'Ha! Ha! Ha!' was painted on a board and 'He! He! He!' on the second. Despite the broad humour, that exhibition was credited with starting the Royal Academy's annual exhibition which opens each May. It also was the spiritual ancestor to a more serious exhibition of pub signs held at the Building Centre in London in 1936 which I mentioned in Chapter Two. The Brewers Society, one of the sponsors of the exhibition, was anxious to leave the depression behind and this was a way to show the bright face of pubs. It was a huge success. Critics said it was 'a minor National Gallery' and as 'nursery rhymes for grown-ups' and the public flocked to see the signs, many of which had been removed from their pubs and brought to London for the exhibition.

One is startled to discover that a member of the aristocracy painted a pub sign. Lady Elizabeth Georgiana (1844–1878), the eighth Duchess of Argyll was also a member of the Royal Academy. She painted the pub sign for the Ferry Inn at Roseneath.

While few pub signs from past centuries still exist, at least one collection of pub sign sketches was recently auctioned. After the death of Lord Clark of Saltwood, Sotheby's, the famous auctioneers, sold his extensive art collection. In the collection was a rare volume of water colour designs for pub signs, circa 1760. The volume is believed to have been a journeyman painter's sample book. The identity of the artist is a mystery although one design bears the signature J. Wootton. The book includes 84 designs, mostly watercolours but some oil paintings as well. The 14 x 10 inch volume was expected to fetch £4000–£6000 but, in fact, was sold for £28,000.

In preparing this chapter, a surprising number of photographs and prints of old pub signs were found. Especially interesting is the page from a 1907 *Illustrated London News* because it carries photographs of pub signs painted by Royal Academicians. Some of these, especially the George and Dragon by Leslie and Hodgson were never known to have been photographed.

There are several fascinating points made clear by these old pictures. First, nothing has changed very much. The carvings of pub signs in the seventeenth century used exactly the same themes and design of painted signs today. Hogarth in the mid-1700s was using humour on his pub sign. And the painted images look much like their modern descendants. There was good art on pub signs in past centuries, painted by artists who would be great or who had already achieved greatness. And that is still happening. Artists who paint pub signs are having exhibitions at the National Portrait Gallery

The Crossed Keys This smithy-made pub sign was crafted of copper and still has some traces of the original gilding. It is now in the Luton Museum although it comes from a pub in St. Albans, Herts. The Crossed Keys as a pub name is very old, dating for the time when most signs had a religious significance. This common sign in Christian heraldry refers to Jesus saying to St. Peter that he would give him the keys to the Kingdom of Heaven.

The Illustrated London News Books about pub signs often refer to signs painted by great English artists of the past. Now, thanks to

this page of photos from the 10 August 1907 issue of the ILN, we can see what they looked like. There is, however, one caveat. All of the pictures were taken by the same photographer and all of the signs appear to be hanging out of doors. Hogarth's sign would have been painted at least 150 years earlier and the George and Dragon at least 30 years earlier. Signs wouldn't normally last that long exposed to the weather. It is possible that the signs had been kept indoors and taken out for these photographs but the text does not say one way or the other. Whatever, it is still a fascinating look at the past.

The upper left photo (1) and upper right photo (3) are two

sides of the sign for the Miller of Mansfield at Goring-on-Thames by Marcus Stone. The Miller of Mansfield was, according to ballad and legend, one John Cockle. Henry II got lost crossing Sherwood Forest. He came upon a miller, John Cockle who made him welcome and gave him some venison to eat. Only the King had the right to hunt deer in the forest but Henry's gratitude outweighed his anger and he knighted Sir John for his services.

The upper middle photo (2) shows the Ferry Inn's sign at Roseneath. It is the only sign known to have been painted by a member of the royalty, The Duchess of Argyll, Lady Elizabeth Georgiana 1844–1878.

The lower left photo (4) is William Hogarth's Man With a Load of Mischief at Blewbury.

The lower right photo (6) shows The Row Barge painted by G. D. Leslie for the pub at Wallingford. Artists painted pub signs for a number of reasons. Many did it to earn money before they were well known, some did it as a favour to a publican, others to pay for their pub consumption.

The centre and bottom centre (5 & 7) are two sides of the George and Dragon at Wargrave-on-Thames. The sign was painted in 1874 and, if it was indeed still hanging some 33 years later, would be understandably worn as it appears to be. G. D. Leslie's side shows the traditional scene of St George slaying the mythical dragon. On the reverse, G. E. Hodgson, 1831–1895, showed St George enjoying a pint after the battle. It is said that they painted the sign to settle their bar bill.

and other venues. Are there artists painting pub signs today who will be considered as great as those in the past? Only time can tell. It is also clear that these artists of the past approached their assignments much as current painters do. These old signs were carefully composed and skilfully painted but with a touch of humour where it seemed appropriate.

Can *any* of the pub signs of the past be seen today? Yes, but not nearly as many as should be available. Most British museums have ignored pubs and pub signs yet it is difficult to understand why. Pubs have been an important part of social history, of the lives of the people, since the days of the Roman occupation, but there is little evidence of this to be seen in the museums.

Indeed, many of the photographs in this chapter which were graciously provided by the museums are of pub signs tucked away somewhere and not on public view.

Fortunately, there are a few places where old pub signs can be seen. Perhaps the best is the York Castle Museum in York, described as England's most popular Museum of Everyday Life. The museum has created a number of rooms, jails, and other scenes of everyday life in past centuries. One of the most popular exhibits is the Kirkgate. This is a spectacular recreation of a nineteenth-century street, courts and alleys. The street is composed of real buildings and building fronts, not 'sets'. Many were collected by a Dr Kirk, after whom the street is named.

The Bull and Mouth In terms of letting us get a look at the past, the Museum of London is a treasure trove. On display in the Museum's nineteenth century gallery is the massive, carved Bull and Mouth sign. This bizarre combination became a pub name when people had trouble pronouncing (or when regulars created a nickname for their local)

The Boulogne Mouth. Why the Boulogne Mouth, itself a strange name for a pub? Probably to honour a naval battle won by Henry VIII's ships in the entrance, the mouth, of Boulogne harbour. Sceptics believe in a more prosaic explanation – that two pubs were combined, as they often have been, and the two names joined together as well.

There are five pub signs on view. On Kirkgate there is the Windmill and its painted sign. The Windmill was a coaching inn and the coach is in front of the inn. There is also the Black Swan on the street and this sign is made of cast iron. On Half Moon Court, depicting life in the first years of this century, is the King William Hotel. In keeping with the growing public literacy, the King William features lettered signs on its windows and an illuminated glass sign. In the Princess Mary Court is a public house and its sign, the Downe Arms. This is a painted wood coat of arms sign. Finally, at York Story, is a guilded wood, the Sea Horse. The particular advantage of the York Castle Museum, in addition to the fact that it has five pub signs on view, is that you can see them in use as they actually looked in the past.

London has a similar museum, the Museum of London, which traces life in London from the Romans to the present. In their nineteenth-century gallery, hung above a doorway, is the massive, carved Bull and Mouth, a famous London pub sign. At present, the museum is renovating and rearranging a number of galleries and hopefully other old signs in its collection will be on view in the future.

The Victoria and Albert Museum in London has two very interesting pub signs on display, but they are a bit hard to find. Make your way to Gallery 48 which is along the Cromwell Road side of the huge museum . . . and look up. Gallery 48 primarily houses the book store and gift shop. Due to lack of space, it was combined with some museum exhibits, primarily old

The Three Kings and **The Three Crowns** Nothing much is known about these two carved pub signs. The Three Kings is made of stone, measures 27 x 26½ x 3½″ and was from London's Lambeth Hill. The Three Crowns was a bit smaller, 21 x 24 x 4½″ and was also from Lambeth Hill. But the signs do tell us a number of things about pub signs in the seventeenth century when these were created. First they were carved signs rather than painted, obviously to last longer in a harsh environment. They were 'patriotic' or perhaps a better phrase is loyal to the Crown. If pub signs could be easily categorized (which they can't be since there are just too many categories to make any easy sense), you could say that two very large groups would be patriotic and religious signs. Another interesting thing about these signs is that they are both in threes. There are a great number of pub names and signs with three somethings. They range from Three Pigeons to Fish to Tuns to Feathers and so on. Three has some mystical significance and has been important in most religions and cultures. Christianity has the Trinity. Three Kings brought gifts to the baby Jesus. The Chinese said that One produced Two, Two produced Three and Three produced everything. Pythagoras said that three was the perfect number having a beginning, middle and end. Taking such a diverse and unorganized number of things such as pub signs, it *is* remarkable that three does seem to dominate and with no central control dictating it.

house fronts. Suspended high above the commercial activity are some pieces of ornamental ironwork and two pub signs. One is a White Hart, painted in the mid-nineteenth century by Miles Birket Foster (1825–1899) and Alfred Cooper, from a pub at Witley, Surrey. The other sign is the Wherryman which was discovered in Norwich and has traditionally been ascribed to Old Crome. The museum dates it as first quarter of the nineteenth century. If it is the same Jolly Sailor, described above, it might be slightly earlier.

The Boar's Head We probably have to thank fourteenth-century Christians for this least-attractive subject for pub signs. They began the practice, still observed at Queen's College, Oxford, of serving a boar's head at a feast. It is a frequently-seen sign. Perhaps part of the attraction is that we have defeated this ferocious beast. This was often the reason for naming pubs The Saracen's Head and putting up a sign showing a frightening fighting man. If the opponent is so terrible, it makes the victory sweeter. This stone carved Boar's Head dates from 1668 and comes from London's Eastcheap.

The artist George Mackenney is one of the finest and most prolific of modern pub sign artists. In other areas, his work as portraitist is exceptional, as shown by this delicate self-portrait.

Seen here at work finishing one of his many signs, his artistry is equally evident in his preliminary sketches, mainly oil on card measuring approximately eight inches by ten inches. On the following pages are many fine examples of such sketches, many of which, despite the elegance of their design were sadly never worked up into finished signs.

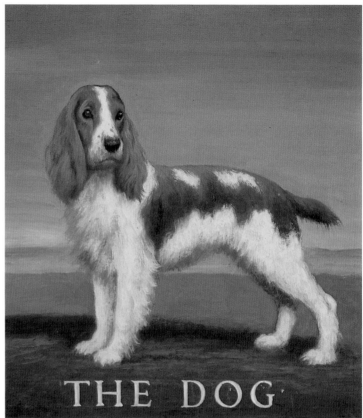

THE DOG

Six Mackenney sketches for pub signs on an animal theme.

Six Mackenney sketches for celestial signs – five 'Suns' and one 'Globe'.

Mackenney's work on human subjects.

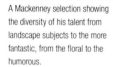

A Mackenney selection showing the diversity of his talent from landscape subjects to the more fantastic, from the floral to the humorous.

Two of George Mackenney's finest sketches – **The Rising Sun** and **The Perseverance**.

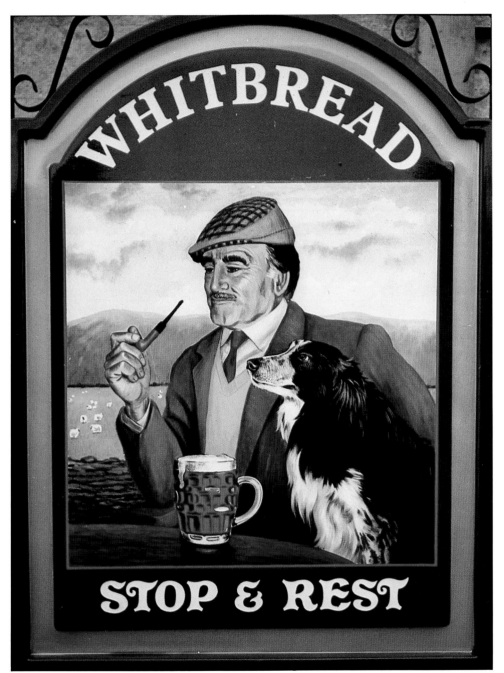

The Stop and Rest This painting uses a number of symbols to reinforce the message: a loving dog; a stream; sheep in the fields on an obviously warm and pleasant day; a pipe and a pint. One trait shared by pub sign artists (part fun and part inspiration) is putting the faces of friends on portrait pub signs. In this case, the unknowing subject is Norman Hartley, founder of Norman Hartley Signs and patriarch of an artistic clan. His son, David, decided that it was time for Dad to be on a sign since he had created so many of them.

The Stop and Rest is a Whitbread pub in Blackburn, Lancashire.

The Shepherd's Rest In these pressured and hurried days, the shepherd has, more than ever, taken on an air of rural peace. No wonder it makes for a good pub sign, promising a restful break from the cares of the day. On pub signs, the shepherd appears with his crook, his dog or his flock but most often, he is alone, sometimes at rest.

The Shepherd's Rest is a Whitbread pub in Roxhill, Hereford. The sign was painted by Brewery Artists.

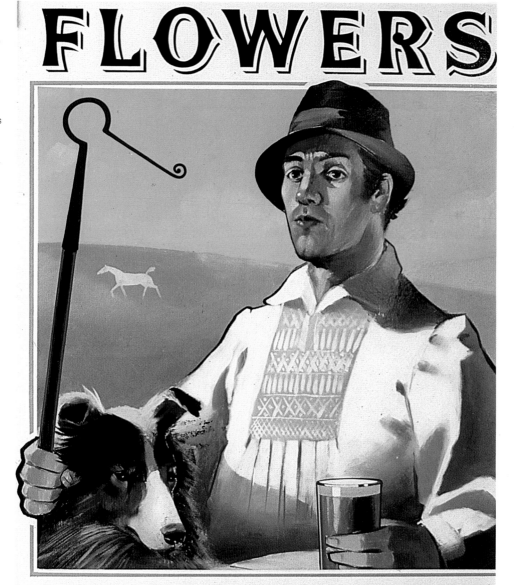

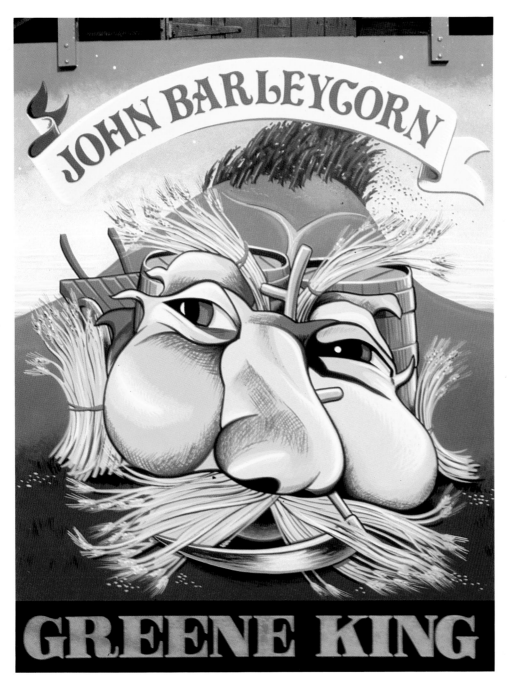

The John Barleycorn Greene King assigned this job to artist Graham Jones and he produced this very imaginative painting, a portrait half human, half implements and barley. The brewery thought it was fine but, unfortunately, the landlady didn't so it was never put up. Luckily Graham received another commission to paint a more straightforward John Barleycorn, which *is* now hanging.

Graham Jones, Douglas Fairbanks and Robin Hood In his garden shed, Graham Jones puts the finishing touches on the face of his Robin Hood. When he received the assignment to paint a Robin Hood pub sign, Graham cast about for a model for his painting. In an old book of cinema publicity pictures, he came across a picture of Douglas Fairbanks, Jr. Mr. Fairbanks was sitting on a chimney on top of a tall building, in New York City with the rest of the skyline behind him. He was posed with a pulled bow, arrow at the ready, to publicize his upcoming appearance in a Robin Hood film. The Fairbanks happy face, with a beard added, made a good model for this pub sign.

The Robin Hood is a Greene King pub in Clifton Reynes which is on the Bedfordshire/ Buckinghamshire border.

The Printers' Devil Since the seventeenth-century, the boys who run errands for printers and do simple tasks while they learn the trade have been called printers' devils. Usually this sign is seen near newspapers or major printing works, in this case the Bristol Evening Post. The rich blend of colours, unusual in pub signs, shows the artistic approach of Paul Gribble.

The Printers' Devil is a Courage pub in Bristol, Avon.

The Imperial Gloucesters This sign shows the members of the Imperial Gloucester Regiment in their traditional battle formation and wearing their traditional uniforms. They are the only regiment to wear their badges on both the front and back of their helmets. This is done because of their basic battle formation, the square, and enables recognition of their comrades from the rear as well as from the front.
The painting is by Stanley Chew.

Stanley Chew, widely recognized as one of the master artists painting pub signs, begins the final work on The Britannia. Stanley works in a small, artist-organized (meaning no one is allowed to touch or move anything but he can put his hand on anything he wants in seconds), cluttered garden shed.

Chapter 4
TODAY'S PUB SIGN ARTISTS

Artists who paint pub signs know a peculiar frustration. Their paintings – in their original state, just as they were painted – are seen by more people than many of the most famous works by the most famous artists. That is because their paintings hang in town centres and on country lanes, along busy main roads and on side streets. But wherever they hang, hundreds and even thousands see them every day. The frustration is that while they are seen by so many, few stop to think about them or wonder who the artist was.

More often than not, pub sign paintings are unsigned. There are a number of reasons for this. The most interesting reason is a rather loose tradition that says you only sign the painting if it is original. Original, in this sense, meaning a new treatment of the name or some other complete change from the former pictorial. It is a loose tradition because there is no organization of pub sign artists, no body of teaching and rarely communication between them. Another and more practical reason is fear of theft. There is a belief, undoubtedly stemming from the days when Hogarth and other greats painted signs, that a sign would be stolen if its artist became famous. And when you realize that, you also realize that they could be stolen a lot easier than if they were in a locked museum or gallery. Yet a third reason is that the signs do hang ten or more feet above the ground and, even if someone wanted to know the artist's name, it would be difficult to read.

Given those frustrations, why on earth would anyone want to be a pub sign artist? The answers are as varied as the artists. Many are commercial sign writers who get into it almost as a sideline. Others enter contests which are occasionally sponsored by breweries or publicans to find a fresh look for a pub. Some go to work in brewery art departments and develop their talents there. But perhaps the most interesting is the academically trained, compulsively productive artist. How and why does he become a pub sign artist?

George Mackenney is a perfect example of a fine artist who has painted a great number of pub signs. He is considered to be the best in the business by many of the major breweries and by other knowledgeable critics and observers. In his career, which has lasted thirty years, he has painted about 6000 pub signs, and, since most signs are two-sided, that means close to 12,000 original oil paintings.

George was born over an East End pub and his father and four uncles were all publicans but he gave no thought to spending his life on anything to do with pubs. He was going to be an artist. To this day, George is a modest man about everything except his talent. He calmly states, 'I enjoy showing off my work because I know I'm good and I can deliver. Also I love what I do. So long as I have a brush in my hand, I paint. I don't care if I'm painting a wall or a portrait as long as I'm painting'.

Studying art not only gave George the fundamentals which would enable him to fully utilize his talents, it also led him to Thelma. Thelma became his wife and partner and the union is still going strong, bolstered by disagreeing about almost everything, after over 50 years. George Mackenney studied art at the Westham School of Art while Thelma was studying at the Hornsey School of Art. It was 1935 and George was ready to take his final examination.

Thelma clearly remembers their first meeting and her first impression of George. 'I was in an all female class and we were painting life studies of a nude model', she recalls. 'George walked in like he owned the place and asked to borrow an easel for his exam.' George adds, 'I was in my Lord Byron period, long flowing hair and a flamboyant blouse. Ahh, I had such beautiful hair back then. I used to shave a bit of it to make a widow's peak'.

George took his borrowed easel and began the painting examination (he had already successfully passed drawing and industrial design) which took 22 days! When the exam was over, George had the equivalent of a First Class Honours.

George approached Thelma again and asked for a date. She said, 'I will go out with you only if you cut your hair'. George cut some off and they had their date. He asked for another and she demanded more hair had to go. That was the end of the Byron period and the beginning of the end of George's bachelor days. They married on 3 November 1935.

Still working as a team with George, Thelma does all of the research as well as the bookkeeping, billing and letter writing. George paints for up to 14 hours a day, only rarely leaving his studio and almost never going on holiday. 'I know people think I'm crazy, but I just love my work,' he says. 'To me work *is* a holiday'.

After art school, George went through a very difficult time. Work was hard to find for a young artist. His belief in his talent unshaken, George (and Thelma) cast around for some other field of art which would satisfy his need to create and yet put food on the table with some regularity. Being an artist and having been born into a pub-oriented family, George was, more than others, aware of pub signs and aware that he could improve on many that he saw. So Thelma wrote letters to 64 breweries asking if they would like George to paint some signs for them. Five said yes, which absolutely delighted the young couple, and a career was born.

From that beginning, came a seemingly endless stream of orders. Through the years, George has painted for virtually all of the major breweries as well as many of the smaller ones and, occasionally, an independently owned pub. From his first sign, the Railway, for Plymouth Breweries, through the 6000 to come, no two signs have been identical except when that is exactly what is wanted. Sometimes a brewery will send George a sign that has been taken down because of weathering or some other damage and insist that he copy it exactly because that is what the publican and/or his customers want. As flattering as that is, George would really prefer the challenge of finding a new way to express an idea, a different way to view a familiar name or theme. Unless it is one of those instances of repeating a sign, a brewery will usually send George the name of one or more pubs and ask for his ideas. This is when the Mackenney team goes into action. George and Thelma live in an early seventeenth-century thatched and half-timbered cottage outside Aylesbury. But inside it is truly a cottage industry. A small, beamed, low-ceilinged room on the first floor is the centre of the activity. It is here that George paints all day and into the evening. In addition to his easel and paints, the room is lined with works in progress and books. Books on all subjects ranging from history to heraldry to bird books and horticulture books to books about artists. There are stacks of magazines on a range of subjects from ships to antiques.

The books are all for research. Piled haphazardly among all of them are notes, sketches, pages torn from newspapers and other reminders of something long forgotten. This is where Thelma starts her job of research. If Thelma can't come up with the right picture or fact there, she goes to one of her outside sources which range from the local library to the British Museum.

George will then paint a sketch or two to illustrate the idea for the new sign. One example George remembers was for a pub called the Shoulder of Mutton. George had done a number of these in the past and prepared one sketch in the normal way, showing the cut of meat. But Thelma's research discovered that King Charles II loved mutton and was known as the 'Mutton Eating King', so George painted a sketch showing the King eating a succulent meal. That became the sign.

'Sketch' is a somewhat misleading term because that can be anything from a pencil sketch to a fully executed oil painting on card. They are usually about 10 inches by 8 inches and are painted on whatever scraps of card George has handy. The sketch is sent to the brewery where up to three or four people give their approval and/or suggest changes. Then the approved sketches are returned to George and he begins the painting. Almost all of those returned sketches are carefully kept to be used as part of the research for future signs.

The signs are painted on wood, plywood, composition board or metal – whatever the brewery wants. Most are now painted on aluminium for its lasting qualities. A helper primes the board and then George, using the same oil paints as he would use for a portrait on canvas, paints the sign. He can do a sign a day but some, like a complicated coat of arms, may take several days. Next he paints (in most cases) a mirror image on the other side of the sign. In some instances, he will paint another version of the same scene. On one side he might paint a farmer going off to the fields in the morning, while the reverse shows him tiredly going home at sunset. Or he might paint the front of a person gathering wheat on one side and the rear view on the reverse. Finally, a special varnish is added to protect the paintings from weather and pollution for as long as possible. 'I guarantee my signs for five years', he said, 'but after that it depends on the conditions. It is very rare for a sign to last more than 10 years'.

If the image is of an historic figure, George and Thelma seek the best portrait from the subject's own time and George bases his work on that, feeling that he has a responsibility for historical accuracy. If the subject is a villain, demon or old and sick he usually paints a self-portrait! Friends' faces as well as any of the half-dozen cats and dogs which share his studio are liable to end up on signs.

Recreation, too, seems to be closely related to his work. George's only physical activity, not counting the standing and painting all day, is a long morning walk. Even that is put to work. About seven years ago, he started painting landscapes for fun. He will often return from his walk, paint a landscape and then get down to working – painting. Classical music, educational programmes on BBC radio or TV keep his mind active in other areas and are his 'holidays' away from painting. About once a month he will take a day away from the easel. Almost always this is for a trip to London to see an exhibition of an artist's work. Finally, of course, there is his great love, portraiture. People come to him, usually through personal recommendation, to have their portrait painted, or their children or their dog or horse. George

Some preliminary sketches by George Mackenney. After these initial pencil pieces, the next step is to produce more finished oil paintings, measuring approximately 8 inches by 10 inches, for submission to the client. Sometimes as many as eight different designs would be required, until one is deemed suitable. (Examples of George Mackenney's oil sketches are illustrated in colour)

mostly fills these commissions on weekends, keeping a five-day schedule for his primary business, pub signs.

Surprisingly, some pub signs can be controversial and provoke heated feelings. Some years ago, George Mackenney was asked by the Charles Wells Brewery to do a new sign for the Adam and Eve. George painted a sign showing the two, unclothed, in the Garden of Eden. The brewery loved it and so did the publican. But some of the neighbours decidedly did not. They found it too graphic – perhaps because Adam and Eve were painted as looking like normal, modern people. The sign came down. George added a few fig leaves, the sign was rehung, and everyone was happy.

Among the other funny things that have happened to George were two cases of mistaken identity – once for being a two hundred year old painter, the other for being George Stubbs. Several years ago, a good friend of the Mackenneys was visiting the area which is now part of the new Milton Keynes and he stopped in an antique shop. There he was offered the opportunity to purchase, for several hundred pounds, an eighteenth-century pub sign, worn but still attractive. He couldn't wait to get back to Aylesbury so he could comment on how long George's career had been. George had painted that eighteenth-century sign just 15 years ago! To add insult to injury, the antique dealer was getting more for the old sign than the £100–£130 breweries pay for each new side.

On another occasion, an acquaintance commissioned George to paint his pet dogs and asked that they be painted in the style of the great George Stubbs. George Mackenney did so, very accurately. The acquaintance moved abroad, forgetting to pay for the painting in the process. Some years later, Thelma opened a magazine and saw an interview with the now well-known man. The accompanying photograph of the subject showed him standing in front of his 'proud possession, a Stubbs original'!

The Central division of Courage Breweries, based in Reading, has a commendable practice. They have the artist (in most cases during the past quarter century it has been George Mackenney) return his sketch to them along with the finished sign. They then write a short narrative about the pub and the origin of its name and something about the sign artist and why he painted the sign the way he did. The narrative and the sketch are then framed and hung inside the pub. Thus, at least in those Courage pubs, the artist gets the recognition he deserves. More breweries should follow Courage's lead.

Another highly successful pub sign artist with a career just about as long as George Mackenney's, although not quite as prolific, is Len Cooper of Cooper Signs in Hertford. Len started painting at age 14 when he became an apprentice in his father's sign painting business. For over 50 years he has been doing the pictorial side of the business as well as some of the regular signage, most of which is now done by his brother John. John also lends a hand on the pictorials so it is sometimes hard to be positive of who has done what on a sign, particularly a repeated one.

With a name like Cooper it must have been almost inevitable that they become involved in pub work since the coopers were the men who made beer barrels. Coopers Signs is in the centre of Hertford's twisting old streets. It is somewhat surrounded by buildings which are part of the McMullens Brewery, an independent brewer operating in Hertford since 1827.

Len Cooper painted this sign of the Jolly Farmers for the McMullens pub in Enfield. This large, comfortable pub is now in a London suburb but probably was so named in an earlier time when this area would have been countryside. Len chose an interesting combination of subjects for this pictorial. One of his Jolly Farmers is still wearing the traditional white smock and is obviously enjoying a pint to a successful day, or more likely to a successful harvest. His companion, sharing a pint and a smile but also making a congratulatory gesture is the landowner, the 'gentleman farmer', the boss. There are many Jolly Something signs with usually no more meaning than to express the good times the pub has to offer. The people being jolly vary from sign to sign depending on location. They may be almost anything – fishermen, butchers, bargemen, woodmen – but usually will give you a clue to the kind of work done nearby now or in the past.

McMullens has about 160 pubs in Hertfordshire, Essex and London. Like other successful independents such as Fuller, Smith and Turner and Samuel Smith, they compete with the bigger breweries by choosing their publicans carefully to ensure friendly, well run pubs. They are also very careful about the pub buildings, signage and especially their pub signs. For many years, Cooper Signs has painted and maintained all of the McMullens pub signs.

This, of course, means that Len Cooper has been able to show his talent and ability on all of them.

In addition to giving a similar style to all of the signs, Len Cooper has been able to display his painting talent and, occasionally, his sense of humour. Now reaching the age where he is beginning to train his successor, he still feels a personal affection for his paintings and speaks of them almost as his children. Len is also engaged in other aspects of the business. He recently completely redesigned and standardized all of the McMullens signage from the typeface used for the brewery name to the designs on walls, mirrors, bar cloths, and so on. In addition to the McMullens work, Len Cooper has been approached to paint signs for other breweries. He doesn't do much of this – due to the pressure of keeping the 160 McMullens signs up to date and in good shape – but he has painted some signs for Courage and Ind Coope.

The Fish and Eels On one side the fish and eels are alive and swimming around while on the other side they have been caught and have expired. This is an unusual sign in that it was painted by two people. It was produced by Sign Design of Clavering. Nominally, the living side was painted by Graham Nicklas and the other by Debbie Grimes, but Graham says that they both actually did parts of both sides!

The Fish and Eels is a canalside Benskins pub in Dobbs Weir, Hoddesdon, Herts.

From the tiny village of Clavering, which is about a 20 minute ride from Saffron Walden in Essex, comes a third source of pub signs. A flourishing company called Sign Design occupies a large first floor over an automobile showroom. When they moved in a few years ago, it was just one great open space, often cold and draughty. Over the years, as time allowed between preparing all kinds of signage, walls have been put up, heating and lighting improved until it is now purpose built space for signwriters and artists.

Sign Design is run by Graham Nicklas, a younger but still quite experienced pub sign artist. Sign Design is primarily in the signwriting business, any sort of signs from simple lettering to imaginative graphics painted on cars, vans, buildings and traditional signboards. Under Graham's direction, the firm has been increasing the number of pub signs it produces, and has become involved in taking down worn or damaged signs (pub signs and lorries seem to be natural enemies, especially in small village streets and winding lanes) then painting, preparing and hanging the new signs. They also become involved in the brackets and posts that support the sign. Graham Nicklas is himself a talented artist but the nature of his operation means he paints less and less these days. Being the boss, he is directing others, getting orders, arranging finances and acting more now as the creative control. Because of this, you can't spot a sign and identify it as coming from Sign Design as you usually can with a George Mackenney. It also means that the art varies from sign to sign. Graham uses both full-time and freelance artists, depending on the work load. Being an independent contractor, Graham and his team have worked for a number of breweries, notably Ind Coope and Ridley's.

A series of unique pub signs resulted from a decision by Websters, a Northern brewery, to make their houses stand out from the rest. They commissioned Kathleen M. Lindsley, an artist who works in wood engravings, to produce a series of signs for them. Kathleen first sketched her design to illuminate each pub name. In some instances, several designs were made, and eventually used, for a single pub. For example, the Woodlands, in Harrogate has several signs showing woodlands in the different seasons, with different animals in each. Kathleen then engraved each design in a piece of wood about the size of a postage stamp – her normal way of working. A black and white print was made of each engraving and then enlarged to the usual pub sign size. Both the style of these excellent engravings and their being black and white gave the Websters pubs a special identity.

Sign Design of Clavering, discussed above, has a lot to look forward to if they can be as successful as Norman Hartley Signs, Ltd. in Manchester. In 1946, artist Norman Hartley struck out on his own and formed a signwriting and painting company. It has become something of a dynasty: Norman, still very active in the company, has been joined by son David and grandson Peter. David is actively involved in managing the whole operation while Peter concentrates on the design side: The Hartleys believe they are the largest producers of pub signs today, producing about 20 per week.

Hartley Signs is a very large organization because it offers the complete service. One department makes the signboards and sprays them with a base coat of paint. Later this department will add any structural or ornamental metalwork to the completed pictorial and prepare it for delivery. A design department has a number of design artists and a very talented cartoonist. Once the designs are made and approved by the brewery (Hartley Signs works for most of the major breweries and many of the regional, independent brewers), the design is sent into the next room, the painting studio. There it will be assigned to one of the staff of artists who paint the pictorials. Once the pictures have been painted on both sides of the board, the sign goes to another room where the signwriters paint on the written words, usually the pub name and the brewery's name. Finally the sign goes back to the preparation group and then to shipping. It will be hung at the pub by a Hartley crew, if so directed, or delivered to the brewery if it has its own installation crew. The results are good because the Hartley family won't have it any other way. Every step of the operation is carefully and

The First-In, Last-Out Like the World's End, the First and Last and other similar names, this pub name has changed its meaning completely. When all travel was by foot or by horse, many people never left the immediate area of their birth, their village or town. In those times, a pub on the edge of the community *was* at the world's end and was the first pub seen on entering and the last seen on leaving the community. Now the name is usually depicted in a funny or lighthearted way. One such pub changed its name to the Cradle and Grave for a while.

For this Cameron's pub in Whitley, Yorkshire, Norman Hartley Signs' artist showed the publican's joy at greeting his first customer and his impatience to be rid of the same man at the end of the session!

thoughtfully controlled so that the resulting signs have a high standard of painting and materials.

Still another source of pub sign art is the brewery artist. This can range from one man who occasionally paints a pictorial to a fully-fledged art department. In the former kind of situation, you find that all breweries have some sort of architect's or property department. There will be at least one employee who prepares lettered signs for the pubs – headings for menu

The Spitfire History can be words in a book and it can also be remembering important things and keeping them alive and in our thoughts. Pub signs, while this is not their prime purpose, can do an excellent job of keeping history alive. This pub is so named because it is where the famous Spitfires, one of the last great propeller-driven fighter planes, were made during World War II. The Norman Hartley Signs' artist painted two views, showing the plane flying and a pilot eagerly scrambling to get his Spitfire aloft.

The Spitfire is a Davenports pub in the Beechcroft Estate, Castle Bromwich, Solihull.

boards, the pub name to be shown outside the pub but not on the sign, announcements, restroom signs, etc. He might also help hang signs and otherwise care for the buildings themselves. Often a person like this will be assigned to paint a pictorial sign, sometimes because of talent, sometimes for expediency.

Brewery Artists, however, is quite different from that almost off-hand approach. A subsidiary company of Whitbread & Co., Brewery Artists is presently located in a building which is part of the Whitbread brewery in Cheltenham but they will soon be expanding and moving to purpose-built quarters. Brewery Artists is what businessmen call a 'profit centre'. That means there is no free ride! Brewery Artists has to sell its work to the various Whitbread companies as well as to other breweries.

Mike Hawkes is the Manager/Chief Artist of Brewery Artists and he has been with the company for 26 years. The group is now eight people strong and will soon expand to add about as many again. Mike says, 'My biggest problem is finding *good* artists. A lot of schools these days turn out students who can't even draw so they go in for abstracts. Pub signs are a demanding

The Sportsman A pub name that can mean almost anything, and it gives the artist great freedom for creativity unless a specific sportsman is to be honoured. In this case it was left to the imaginations at Brewery Artists and they took a light-hearted, cartoon approach showing, on each side of the sign, the pitfalls of sport. Probably since most artists seem to be nature-loving people, animals fare very well on pub signs. They are usually depicted getting the better of humans or of the usually victorious, hunting animals: the mouse fools the cat, the fox beats the hounds and all animals confound humans!

The Sportsman is a Whitbread pub in Stratford upon Avon, Wiltshire.

The Admiral Hardy The artists at Brewery Artists are not only successful when painting peaceful scenes of country shepherds but equally talented portraying real people. This portrait sign shows Thomas Masterman Hardy, 1769–1839. Hardy was born in Dorset and first served under Nelson as a

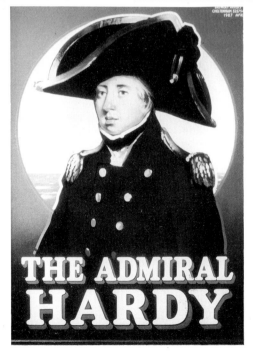

lieutenant. He was promoted to captain after the Nile. He commanded the Victory during the blockade of Toulon until Trafalgar. Thomas Hardy died an Admiral and Governor of Greenwich Hospital.

The Admiral Hardy is an Eldridge Pope & Co. pub in Weymouth, Dorset.

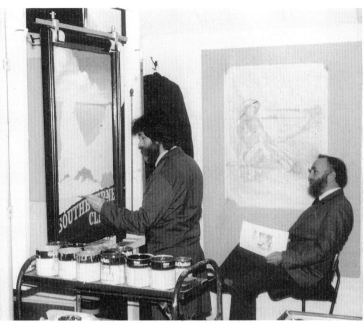

This photo shows two members of Brewery Artists, the Whitbread subsidiary, at work. Rob Rowland is painting at the easel while Manager and Chief Artist Mike Hawkes watches. The staff of Brewery Artists has developed and evolved a unique easel. It is a vertical frame which firmly clasps the framed board. It can be raised, lowered or reversed with the touch of a finger. This makes it easy to work directly on any part of the board and to do both sides of the sign at the same time. About six feet behind Rob is a mirror attached to the ceiling and angled down toward the easel. The painter frequently looks over his shoulder, thus seeing his painting reversed and at a distance. If anything is wrong, it is then quickly apparent. George Mackenney will often turn a completed painting upside down to get the same new perspective and error-check. Mike is holding the original pencil sketches for the sign which had been used to get approvals for the design. An enlarged version of the sketch is pinned to the wall to guide the artist. On the easel behind the one Rob is painting on is a partially completed pictorial. The background has been painted in and is being left to dry. Brewery Artists use Dulux exterior paints rather than artists' oil paints because they feel these paints stand up to the weather longer.

kind of art. You have to be able to create an accurate likeness, a bright and eye-catching painting. That's what it's all about'.

Like Hartley Signs and Sign Design, Brewery Artists has to 'sell' its product, even to Whitbread and often in competition with other artists and design companies. But Mike and his team also have the freedom to sell their services outside the company. This, they feel, helps them stay out of a rut, stay competitive and, perhaps most important, it constantly challenges them artistically. Some of the other brewers they have worked for are Ansells, Eldridge Pope and Morlands. And, again, like independent design firms, they provide a complete package of sign, framing, hanging, signwriting and so on, sometimes using sub-contractors. They also get the odd special job. Recently the U.S. Airforce came to them for help with a huge, blank and unattractive hangar. The hangar was big enough to hold one of the giant tanker aircraft used in mid-flight refuelling. So, on this giant blank wall, they painted a tanker, almost full-size, coming in for landing.

Independent but closely linked to one brewery is an artist named Graham Jones. In a sense, he represents the freelance artists who paint for one smaller brewery. Typically, such a brewery might not want the expense of having an in-house artist but will so like the work of one person that they will give him or her all of their work. Since their tied pubs might number from less than 100 to several hundreds, one artist can handle all or most of their requirements. Graham Jones does most of the Greene King Brewery's pub signs .

Graham Jones works from his home in Bedford. He does perform commissions other than pub signs, but pub signs are becoming an increasingly important part of his output. Among many other lessons he has learned is, he says, 'to work fast! I no longer have the luxury of sitting and waiting for inspiration, I have deadlines to meet! Pub sign art gives me a good living but only if I work hard at it.' His words are echoed by other artists, like George Mackenney. Pub sign artists must produce constantly and efficiently if they are to turn out the volume of work needed to make a good living.

Graham Jones works in an unbelievably (to the observer) small garden shed behind his home. It is about 8 feet long by 4 feet wide. The entrance is blocked by pub signs drying and primed boards waiting to be painted. Graham actually paints at one end of the shed with light provided by good-sized windows. His inspiration comes from his imagination, from books and from the faces of friends. Like other artists, he will sometimes use friends' faces unless he is portraying an actual, historical person. Greene King, for its part, is happy to have an artist of Graham's talent who will specialize in its work and who can be depended on to produce to meet its deadlines.

Yet another variation of the relationship between brewery and artist is represented by Paul Gribble. Paul is an artist who loves to paint railroad trains and has been elected a member of the Guild of Railway Artists. His paintings of trains are so popular that they are reproduced as posters and, just recently, as commemorative plates.

Paul works in his house in Bristol where he executed most of his commissions. He will, if it is appropriate (as it often is with trains) paint on site as well. Paul can't really remember how he got started painting pub signs. He likes the challenge of the necessary boldness of pub signs and the freedom to interpret a pub name in a fresh, creative way. He has, so far, painted for several breweries, including Courage and Bass Charrington. His paintings have a wonderful richness and almost seem drenched with strong colours.

It is appropriate to conclude this look at the artists who paint pub signs with one who is also considered a 'Grand Master' of pub sign artists. Conversation with artists, design companies and brewers all around Great Britain almost invariably include two names. First, George Mackenney and in the same breath, Stanley Chew is named. Oddly, Stanley Chew and George Mackenney have never met although each knows the other's work very well. And they could be, in some senses, 'twin brothers'. Both are over 70, both had formal art training, both sort of backed into pub sign art, both are bearded, they happily live in beautiful surroundings and both could be called, in the politest sense combatitive. While George loves to argue with Thelma and a variety of friends, Stanley loves to take on the establishment when he thinks they are wrong. Finally, of course, both are wonderful Artists!

Stanley Chew was, at the time, the youngest student ever accepted at the Royal College of Art. But his training was curtailed by The Second World War and Stanley became a soldier. Art was, for the duration of the war and some time after, set aside. Stanley married, had children, began doing farm work and established his home in Croft Cottage, a lovely old home on the banks of the River Dart in Buckfastleigh, Devon. Suddenly, at age 42, he lost his job because the farming operation he was working at decided to change their method of operation. Casting about to find a new way to earn a living and keep his home, he found pub sign painting and hasn't looked back. For some 30 years he has produced excellent pictorials for a variety of breweries

The Woolsack The law lords sit on woolsacks for the official opening of parliament. In this pub sign, Stanley Chew has exercised his subtle sense of humour. He portrayed the woolsack supporting the Crown and the Law. And by adding the shepherd's crook he is showing that the whole thing is supported by the common man.

The Woolsack is a Courage pub in Weston Super Mare, Avon.

like Bass, Courage and Whitbread.

Stanley, like Graham Jones, works in a separate shed a few yards from his house. His shed is about double the size of Graham's but still crowded and, to the observer, a very close place in which to produce such fine art. But Stanley is happy here. It is his personal kingdom, he knows where everything is and no one dares 'clean-up' the place. Unlike most artists, he wisely started photographing his work many years ago and has a valuable record of it. Knowing that so many would be destroyed by the weather, at least he has the photographs.

Stanley Chew will speak his piece if he thinks something is wrong. His most recent battles are to keep the River Dart clean and unpolluted, a campaign which even saw him showing 'his' river and his efforts to protect it on independent television. Stanley Chew makes the point also heard from George Mackenney and other independent artists. He says, 'I paint for my living. I don't want to stop because I love my work. But I also can't stop. There is no pension, no big bank account. So I'll keep on painting as long as they let me!'

One characteristic of Stanley Chew's art is his careful use of light and dark. He paints always to make the central figure or object stand out clearly from whatever else is in the painting. And he does this with subtle shadings and graduated use of colour. The characteristics he shares with other great artists of pub signs is his obvious talent and the sense of humour he injects, subtly or broadly, whenever he feels it will make a better pub sign.

One final example shows just how varied pub sign art can be. There is a

pub off London's Fleet Street called the Cartoonist. It is the headquarters and frequent meeting place of the Cartoonist Club of Great Britain. Once, every other year, the pub sponsors a contest for club members to choose a new sign, drawn by a cartoonist!

The artists described in this chapter, while certainly among the best pub sign artists (in fact among the best artists of any kind), represent many others. These are artists whose work or reputation led to them being included. Other artists are represented in this book and their stories are not being told in any detail to avoid repetition. There are many artists not included in this book only for reasons of space or the author's ignorance of their work. To them, too, a vote of thanks for the pleasure they give each day to those who stop and look.

The total number of pub sign artists in Great Britain is not known and

The Fox For at least four centuries the Fox has been a favourite pub sign. Today it does not appear in cities but is still to be found in the country, especially in fox hunting areas. The fox is often found in combination with other animals, most notably with hounds. It is often shown in a humorous light, particularly outwitting the hounds in one way or another. This alert and attractive fox was painted by Paul Gribble for a pub but has never been hung up – the pub went through a name change.

The Victoria Sadly, this very appealing Stanley Chew painting was never hung outside the pub for which it was painted as the pub ran into planning permission problems. Stanley's painting shows Queen Victoria when she was just a four-year-old princess, based on the famous S. P. Denning portrait. Usually pubs called the Victoria have signs showing the Queen in her later years or as the younger woman when she married Prince Albert.

The Luckwell When Stanley Chew was commissioned to paint a pub sign for the Luckwell, he was unable to discover why the pub had been called the Luckwell so, he decided on a realistic painting filled with symbols of good luck. There are four – the horseshoe, Magpies, a black cat, and four-leaf clovers. Stanley, wisely, chose two for his painting. The bird, incidentally, was originally named the Pie but, because of its antics, got the nickname Maggoty. Maggoty and Pie became magpie.

The Luckwell is a Bass pub in the Luckwell section of Bristol, Avon.

probably can never be known. Since they range from George Mackenney, arguably the best and most prolific, to a young artist who wins a contest and paints one sign and never does another, there is no organization, no register of pub sign artists. And that is one of the factors in making this such a fascinating study – the art of the pub sign is unreservedly varied. Signs are mostly bright, bold, relatively simple and about 4 feet by 3 feet. Within those parameters, it is as wide open an art form as is possible.

The Duke of York King Edmund created the title of Duke of York in 1385 and there have been many so-named dukes since. Richard Duke of York's claim to the throne led to the War of the Roses. There is a well-known song about George III's second son, Frederick August, The Grand Old Duke of York which led to this interpretation. The song referred to his commanding the English army in Flanders in 1794–95 but, in truth, there were no hills for him to lead men up and down. Artist Gaye Lockwood made a visual joke with this sign, showing

the troops climbing up his hat on one side and down his hat on the reverse of the sign.

The Duke of York is a Tolly Cobbold pub.

Chapter 5

THE FUNNY SIDE OF THE SIGN

A pompous art critic would say that pub sign art is not serious art, meaning not to be considered for its art value. He'd be both right and wrong. Pub sign art ranges from dreadful to magnificent, just as do the paintings in galleries and museums. But pub sign art is definitely not serious. It rarely takes itself seriously and it is frequently deliberately funny, sometimes unintentionally funny.

Belloc said, 'When you have lost your inns drown your empty selves for you will have lost the last of England'. Whilst he was talking about all of the welcoming and hospitable aspects of pubs, part of that is humour. By their nature, pubs generate good feelings and good humour and that carries through onto the signs.

Again Hogarth comes immediately to mind with his 'A Man Loaded with Mischief' which was not exactly flattering to wives or women in general. Women have often been the target for pub sign humour. A headless woman or a woman holding her head underneath her arms has been painted on any number of signs down through the centuries, illustrating the pub name the Silent Woman or the Quiet Woman. A third version of this was even printed in gold on the cover of that serious 'bible' of signs, Larwood and Hotten's *History of Signboards*, printed in London in 1866. It shows a sign of a headless woman with the name the Good Woman. In a similar vein is the Nag's Head showing a horse's head on one side and a screeching woman's head on the reverse.

Any feminists reading this please note: do not contact a lawyer because the lawyers fare just as badly. The Good Lawyer and the Honest Lawyer are either shown holding their hand neath their arm or peering through bars. They were natural targets for rough humour as are the barmaids of today. It was the ale wife who served the beer and, if the brew was bad, it was she who got the abuse or the ducking in the pond. So while many such signs can be attributed to the male chauvinist pig (and there certainly should be such a pub sign!), the tradition is older and less sexist.

Another traditional pub name and sign pokes fun at a bigger group of stereotypes. The Five Alls usually shows five portraits, side by side, showing a king, a bishop, a lawyer, a soldier and an unhappy man. The legends under the portraits say I Rule All, I Pray For All, I Plead for All, I Fight for All and I Pay for All! An occasional variation of this is the Six Alls with a devil added saying I Take All. A similar sign in intent is the Triple Plea which shows a dying man in bed surrounded by a parson, a doctor and a lawyer . . . and a waiting, smiling devil.

There are many other examples of such humorous signs where the pictorial is the result of the pub's humorous name. One such is the Pig and Whistle which in present days is one of those pub names with a variety of explanations for the name. Some say it comes from the Saxon *piggin* which meant pail and *wassail* referring to the bowl and/or the toast. Others say it comes from *pig-washail* a Saxon toast meaning 'health to the girls'. Yet a third explanation is that pig comes from peg since there was a time when a large tankard was passed around. The side was lined with pegs, indicating how much one should drink as the tankard was passed to him. 'Taking him down a peg' meant the others in the circle drinking more than one share each to thus deprive the 'wrongdoer' of his peg or share.

The Case is Altered gives artists the chance to use their imagination as

The Eager Poet Pub sign artists can be guilty of the worst puns imaginable. There was the Lute and Tun sign at Luton and Bull and Mouth signifying Boulogne Mouth, where there was a famous naval battle. It might help understand this sign if you know that the pub is in Milton Keynes. The poet is Milton, looking keen.

The Eager Poet is a Whitbread pub in the Eaglestone area of Milton Keynes, Bucks.

The Tipsy Gent What do you do when you buy a newly-free freehouse in a re-emerging part of Birmingham to attract and build regulars? That was the task facing the new owners of the Gipsy Tent. First they refurbished the pub inside and out and then had a bright idea. With a change in just two letters of the pub's name, they could get some publicity and give the pub a friendly, raffish personality. So was born the Tipsy Gent and now the basic skills of making customers welcome and serving good beers and food have started the pub on the road to being an excellent local.

The Tipsy Gent is a Freehouse on Cherrywood Road, Bordesly Green area of Birmingham, serving the Wolverhampton and Dudley Breweries' Bank's beers.

The Three Pigeons These are peculiar looking pigeons; they are vultures. Why does a pub called the Three Pigeons have Three Vultures on its sign? To publicize the pub at the time of an extensive refurbishment. There has been a pub on the site since the 1600s and it was a famous coaching inn. It still is but these days the coaches arrive on rubber wheels. The Three Pigeons is the site of what was reported to be the last hanging of a Highwayman. It seems that the unfortunate thief came into the Three Pigeons to celebrate his robbery – but so did his victim. The thief was recognized, caught, tried and hanged in the garden, all in the proper sequence, of course.

The Three Pigeons is a Halls Oxford and West pub just off the M40 at Milton Common, Oxon.

well. It has appeared as an unhappy lawyer, a frightened priest or a building on a hill! Those illustrations go with the various theories of the name. First, that it comes from a lawyer upon hearing surprise evidence that goes against his client saying, 'Well, the case is altered.' Or, if you prefer, it originally meant Casey's altar. This story says that Fr Casey, a Catholic priest during a time of persecution, set up his altar and said Mass in the pub. Or it was said by a publican about his trade when the soldiers who had been billeted nearby went off to fight Napoleon. Or it referred to a Spanish inn which was on top of a high hill and known as La Casa Alta.

An odd name which gives a lot of freedom in painting the sign but, in this case, rarely tries to capture the original meaning, is the World Turned Upside Down. This has variously been attributed to convicted prisoners being sent off to Australia, the tune played by the British army band after defeat by the upstart Americans and to any number of local upsets. Artists usually take this opportunity to let the animal kingdom get its own back at man's expense. One such shows a donkey riding in a cart pulled by a man. Another depicts dogs ridden by foxes and chasing a man. Yet a third shows a mouse chasing a terrified cat.

A last example is the Labour in Vain which is normally portrayed as a woman scrubbing a coloured child in a tub and looking bewildered when she can't scrub him white. These have all been examples of pubs with odd names which gave the artists freedom to have some fun. But one pub name so often stumps artists that the sign simply appears as words or as a large question

Silks You would have to be quick to enjoy this new sign for a pub in Bristol. The pub is in the court area and popular with solicitors and barristers. The pub was formerly named the Malt and Hops but was renamed Silks in 1984, a reference to legal robes. This new sign, showing a leggy lady wearing a barrister's wig, black stockings and high heels, was put up in February of that year. By November the outraged complaints of female lawyers were still raging so the sign came down. It was replaced by a more sedate one. The original Silks sign was auctioned for charity.

Pub signs have a remarkable ability to arouse strong emotion and opinions, particularly at the time of the Commonwealth when signs became very political. This was the case of the Rose which had to be taken down when Charles II was out of power but, when he was restored to the throne, it came back as the Rose Revived.

The Piddle Inn, Piddletrenthide, Dorset. Carried away by the River Piddle!

mark. That is the Who'd a Thought It?, often so called because most of the locals doubted that the landlord would ever get a licence.

Another kind of humorous illustration happens when the artist takes an otherwise straight pub name and gives it a funny treatment. One Builder's Arms shows a contented working man with six arms, two are laying bricks, two hold a book and a sandwich and the last two hold a hand of cards and a pint of beer – no wonder he looks so contented! At least one Old Red Lion is shown as an old, tired, white-bearded red lion sitting down and resting against a barrel of beer.

The Fox and Hounds is treated both seriously and humorously. These signs often show the fox outsmarting the hounds, hiding behind a wall or perched atop a sign whilst the hounds run by. One marvellous George Mackenney sign shows two foxes dressed in hunting pinks seated at a pub table being served their drinks by an aproned hound. These signs, by their nature, make the animals almost like those in cartoons with human expressions of fear or frustration. More subtly, many signs of animals have that slight humanizing touch that makes them more appealing than a straight animal portrait. Quirley animal signs are an echo, probably an unconscious one, of the medieval interest in 'the world turned upside down'. On the misericords (wooden seats which fold down, in the choirs of major churches) there are carvings which show cats vanquishing dogs; mice menacing cats; dogs chased by hares, and many similar designs.

Humour can be intentional, as in the examples above. Often, though, the amusing qualities of a sign's design may be completely unexpected. A design can seem perfectly straightforward to its creator, only to lead to complications of one sort or another. George Mackenney tells two funny stories of his pub sign paintings that never did see the light of day. He was asked by one brewery to submit a sketch for a new treatment for a pub called the Good Intent. This seemed an opportunity for a good pun, and George thought of a number of possibilities before he alighted on the design he submitted. George sketched a soldier, kneeling and praying in the opening of a tent on the eve of battle. The soldier was Cromwell. The good in a tent. The sketch was rapidly rejected and returned . . . the Good Intent pub is in an Irish section of London – not an area to appreciate Cromwell in any form!

The King's Arms The coat of arms beautifully carved on the front of the building and repeated on the sign of the King's Arms is, in fact, that of Queen Anne. No one now remembers why the pub has inaccurately named itself and it has been wrong for so long now that everyone is happy to let the inaccuracy be part of the charm.

The King's Arms is a freehouse in Berkhamsted, Herts.

Just over a year ago, landlord Paul Gallant of the Oat Sheaf in Fleet was asked by the brewery architect in charge of refurbishing the pub what kind of new sign he wanted. 'I jokingly said it should have a naked woman gathering the oat sheafs', he recalls, 'and promptly forgot all about it'. The brewery gave the job to George Mackenney and George painted it. Although he was sure it would never get hung, George painted one side of the sign showing a nude girl gathering the oats and the backside of the sign showed, shall we say, the backside of the scene. The plates were delivered and Paul Gallant, took one look and discreetly hid them. But he added, 'I showed them to my wife and she went through the roof'. So, as expected, back to George to add clothing. But George liked them so much that he kept them and painted a completely new sign for the pub.

Then, of course, there is the unintentional humour of a pub sign that is just plain wrong. There is an historic freehouse in Berkhamsted, Herts called the King's Arms. This 300 year old pub has seen its share of royalty including Queen Anne and Queen Victoria. King Louis XVIII of France was a frequent visitor during his exile in England, partly because he was quite taken with one of the publican's daughters. The front of the pub features a relief carving of the coat of arms set into the brickwork on the first floor. The only problem is that it is the coat of arms of Queen Anne! The error has been known for many years but has become part of the pub's tradition and no one wants to change it in any way.

Pub sign art is not serious art. Thank heaven!

Chapter 6

HISTORY LIVES ON SIGNS

AN EXPLANATION OF PUB NAMES

The title of this chapter uses the word history loosely because there is a strong element of folklore and error in pub signs. Folklore, because that is the source of explanations as to why pubs have the names they do and why pub signs show the images they do, and error because, whilst most artists and breweries work very hard to be historically accurate, mistakes are sometimes made and then perpetuated because they become popular. Such is the case of the King's Arms described in the chapter on humour. Also one finds that meanings change in the course of time. 'Endeavour' was the name of the ship that took Captain Cook on his voyage of discovery to Australia. Much more recently and just 200 years after Captain Cook's journey, the Endeavour was the Apollo 15 spaceship that went to the moon. Endeavour, of course, also means to strive, to work hard. So a pub with that name could have at least three different signs over the years. (The Endeavour in Chelmsford solves the problem by showing the ship on one side of its sign, the spaceship on the other). So, while trivia lovers may go around Britain looking to 'collect' all the kings and queens, famous battles, ships, etc., care or a willingness to accept unintentional substitutes is necessary!

As you travel, you may wonder about some pub signs and pub names. It is, after all, the pub's name that the pub sign artist has to interpret. Here then are some of the most interesting names and their origins. This is an eclectic list and will certainly not cover every pub name or even every unusual pub name. Many pub signs (such as Fox, Princess Louise, Shears, White Horse, etc.) have origins which are usually easily determined. And while most of the following appear on a number of signs, a few individual ones are included just because they are good stories.

Adam and Eve The parents of us all appear on many signs. Obviously, many pubs first used this as a name with religious meaning. Adam and Eve were also constant characters in medieval morality plays and mysteries, thus spreading their popularity. In 1591, they became the central figures in the arms of the Fruiterers Company. They are also supporting figures in the arms of the Company of Needlemakers, so pubs with a relationship with either trade might also use this name. Perhaps the most appropriate Adam and Eve is at Paradise, in the Cotswolds.

Albion This ancient and poetic name for England is gaelic in origin. Legend says this son of Neptune discovered England and ruled it for about a half century. Another story is that Albion was a Roman and, having come to Britain became the first Christian martyr here.

Alls, the Three, Four, Five or Six In its original medieval form, this was the Three Alls, three portraits representing a monk, 'I pray for All', a knight, 'I fight . . .' and a commoner, 'I work . . .'. Later a monarch was added 'I rule' and later still a lawyer 'I plead'. The modern versions show a monarch, a priest, a lawyer, a soldier and an ordinary citizen or John Bull (either 'I work for all' or 'I pay for all'). The occasional sixth? The devil, 'I take All'.

Alma Many different pictorials are used to illustrate this battle of the

Crimean War. Some pubs bearing this name have direct connections with that war, having been founded by a veteran or having seen a son go off to fight. Others took the name to honour the victory. Occasionally, the sign shows a woman, either a portrait of a specific Alma or just a generalized portrait.

Anchor No doubt you would think this is a nautical sign, but this was originally used as a religious sign, as it is the Christian symbol of the virtue of Hope. Thus the Hope and Anchor is really a visual form of tautology. But it often makes a beautiful sign with Hope being shown as a white gowned woman. Later the Anchor became obviously associated with sailors' pubs. When the Pilgrims landed in America (at the wrong place, incidentally – they were heading for Virginia but landed at Plymouth Rock because they were running out of beer and other necessities) their first words were 'We Anchor in Hope'.

Angel In a sense, this is a case of pubs being named after a sign. The very first paintings of angels hung over pubs represented the Archangel or St Michael, the patron saint of military men such as the Knights Templar, who would put such paintings over a pub not to name it but to show it was under God's protection. The angel was an easily recognizable symbol which became a name when people shortened 'at the sign of the angel' to 'the Angel' when referring to the pub. Some years ago, a pub sign artist painted an angel holding a tankard with a halo over it for a pub at Braintree in Essex. The local vicar was not amused and proclaimed it disgraceful.

Arms There is an endless variety of pub signs bearing coats of arms. These come from three main sources. First, a pub might take the arms of the local landowner who owns or owned the land or of a nearby family. Then there are the arms of trade, guild, military or school groups, etc. Finally, there are the arms of royalty, the most popular of the coats of arms signs. Sometimes a pub will show a coat of arms even when its name is not the Something Arms. For example, the Duke of York might show the arms rather than the man. Associated with this are the again countless signs with heraldic symbols (see the Red Lion, below, the most popular pub sign of all). When King Richard II declared that all pubs must have signs, in 1393, those pubs which didn't have a name or a sign often took the White Hart from the King's arms.

Artichoke Probably the artichoke only came into popularity as a pub name and sign because it was a scarce novelty. When it was first introduced to Britain it was imported from Sicily and cost a 'crowne a piece'. It became a symbol for a gardener and for pubs in garden areas.

Axe & Compass The Axe appears in the arms of the Coopers and Wheelwrights Companies. The compasses normally refer to masons and joiners. The axe and compass also appear in the arms of the Company of Carpenters. Thus, whatever the story in an individual pub, this name represents working men.

Bag O' Nails As with many signs, there is a choice of meaning. One origin for this name is that it is a corruption of Bacchanals with its connotations of drunken revelry. The more prosaic is that it refers to an artisan, perhaps an ironmonger and was first used when such an artisan became a publican.

Bear and Ragged Staff This was the crest of the Nevilles, the Earls of Warwick. It may indirectly trace its popularity to performing bears in side shows and the barbaric 'sport' of bear baiting.

Beehive Certainly this is sometimes related to beekeeping but it also is related to wax chandlers. It is a general symbol of business and hard work. Some pubs include an inscription on the sign:
> 'Within this hive we're all alive
> Good liquor makes us funny;
> If you are dry, step in and try
> The flavour of our honey.'

Beetle & Wedge In this case, a beetle is the heavy hammer used to drive in a wedge so this was a sign associated with builders and shipwrights.

Bell Even now if you see a pub with this sign, look around for a church. This ancient sign originated with pubs attached to or near early churches. In early times, it was believed that the sound of a bell could protect the listener from harm by lightning or storm. The English have always been known for their love of bells – Handel said it was the national musical instrument. Bells come in numbers on pub signs varying from one to twelve. Eight Bells is very popular because it is the usual number of peals and blue seems to be the most popular colour, perhaps because it is the colour of hope.

Bird in Hand A popular sign, usually from a family crest or some association with falconry. But there is also the proverb 'A bird in the hand is worth two in the bush' which may have come from a nearby pub being the Bush!

Bishop's Head While it seems illogical, this was once an anti-religious sign or perhaps anti-papist is more correct. At the time of the Reformation, many pubs with 'religious' names were busy changing their names and signs to secular, safe ones. So the Pope's Head regularly became the King's Head and the Crossed Keys lost their association with St Peter and became the keys of a watchman. So too did some Pope's Heads and Cardinal's Heads become the less controversial Bishop's Heads.

Black Bull For some reason, the Black Something (bull, dog, lion, boy, etc.) is a popular pub sign colour. While this sign has obvious connections with the animal, it was once an indication of a Yorkist, a supporter of George, Duke of Clarence, because it appears on his coat of arms.

Black Dog This sign is interesting because its origin is obscure; it has no heraldic significance as does the Talbot. One interesting speculation is that it represents the Devil, who is sometimes called the black dog or supposedly appears as one. Also, interestingly some refer to a hangover or depression as being in the clutches of the black dog.

Black Lion A very old pub sign and name, it comes from the arms of Edward III's queen, Phillipa of Hainault, who was Flemish. Similarly the Golden Lion and Fleur de Lys have foreign heraldic origins, relating to France.

Blue Anchor The Anchor (see above) is the symbol of hope and blue is her emblematic colour. Some Blue Anchors are blue to distinguish themselves from nearby Anchors of different colours but blue is also quite a favourite colour on pub signs and in the names of pubs.

Blue Bells See Bells

Blue Boar The boar, being a familiar wild animal as well as an heraldic device, appears on many pub signs. The White Boar was Richard III's crest and because of it he was known as the 'hog'. It is said after the battle of Bosworth in 1485, many White Boars became Blue Boars because that was the crest of his enemy, the Earl of Oxford, a supporter of Henry Tudor.

Blue Posts Prior to the numbering of houses, which took place in London in the 1760s, people painted the doors or door posts of their house as a means of identification and for giving directions. This practice is thought to date back to Roman times.

Boar's Head As mentioned above, the boar was a well known animal and, therefore, a good sign in illiterate times. But the Boar's Head was also from the arms of St Blaise, the patron saint of weavers and woolcombers.

Bottle and Glass See Tankard

Bull See Bull and Mouth

Bull and Mouth The most enjoyable story of this name is that it is a corruption of Boulogne Mouth and commemorates a naval victory of Henry VIII there. A more prosaic explanation and probably the correct one is that it dates from the combining of two pubs, the Bull and the nearby Mouth, near Aldersgate in London. The bull has always been a very popular pub sign due to its recognizability and its popularity as a working animal. Some pubs with Bull in their name also stem from a religious source because bull also comes from '*bulla*', an ecclesiastical seal.

Butchers Arms Many artisans like butchers, miners, bricklayers, and blacksmiths do not generally possess arms but in the late eighteenth century, pub signs began 'ennobling' them. Perhaps this is why there are often humorous signs depicting their physical arms as opposed to their heraldic arms.

Cardinal's Head See Bishop's Head

Case is Altered A sign with myriad possible reasons for it being chosen. A lawyer told a farmer that if his cows got into a neighbour's turnips the farmer

This **Seven Stars**, a Friary Meux pub in Leigh, Redhill, Surrey, had a special reason for the pictorial. The pub is at least as old as 1637 because, when redecorating, they found painted on a wall, "Gentlemen you are welcome to sit at your ease, pay what you call for and drink what you please", signed William Eades, 1637. Being that old a pub, it does have many low beams and, in fact, a low entrance doorway. One regular inevitably walks into the doorway beam so the landlord asked artist Karen Boswell to paint him doing so and seeing the seven stars.

George Mackenney exhibits his humour in this treatment for **The Hare and Hounds**.

The Cartoonist The Cartoonist is a pub near London's Fleet Street which celebrates the art of cartoonists. The pub is the meeting place for the Cartoonists Club of Great Britain. Once a year the Club votes for the person who has given them the most inspiration during the year and invites him or her to a celebration at the pub.

Every two years the Club votes for a member to design and paint a new sign for the pub. The current sign was painted by Mike Payne. While many signs are painted in a cartoon style, this is believed to be the only pub sign honouring cartoonists themselves.

The Cartoonist is a Chef and Brewer pub on Little New Street, just off Fleet Street, London.

The Rising Sun The sun, the moon and the stars have always been very popular as pub signs. The reasons for this are almost as many and as varied as the ways in which they are depicted. First, there is a very practical reason – they are easy to paint. There is also a better reason. The naming of early pubs was often an expression of faith or a prayer for success and protection. The sun, and particularly the rising sun, was considered to be happy, to relate to new beginnings. In some cases The Rising Sun is shown as here in a humorous fashion. This is the kind of sign that brings a smile even to passersby.

The Rising Sun is at Aston Clinton and is a Courage pub. The sign was painted by George Mackenney whose work and life are described in Chapter 2.

The Mousetrap One of those names which lead to speculation – was the pub so-called because it once had a mouse problem which it solved successfully? Whatever the original inspiration, artist Stanley Chew was given free reign to come up with a humorous sign. In this, he has painted a double joke. We first laugh at the mouse carefully stealing the cheese while his wife looks on worriedly. But wait, his tail is going to be caught when the trap springs! No, Stanley painted an arch in the trap wire so the tail will escape by a whisker.

The Mousetrap is a Bass Charrington Pub in Bourton-on-the-Water, Oxfordshire.

The publican at the **Oatsheaf** in Fleet was only joking when he told the brewery architect that he wanted his new sign to show a naked girl gathering the oats. The architect told George Mackenney and that is just what George painted, front and rear! George knew it probably would not see the light of day. It was returned so that she could be dressed but, by then, George was so fond of the paintings that he kept them and painted a whole new sign, properly dressed, of course.

Pub Signs

These miniature pub signs are part of a set of 50 issued by Whitbread about 50 years ago. Miniature pub signs have been used in promotions several times. Usually the little signs are printed on cardboard, much like cigarette cards, but this set was printed on tin, each measuring 3" x 2", to be collected at Whitbread pubs in Kent and Sussex. The front of each showed the sign and the pub name and location, the reverse gave more details of the address and listed the name of the pub sign artist – unusual but welcome recognition for the artists.

95

An observant traveller along the A4 heading out of London to the West might be startled by seeing a pub with two signs just before the Chiswick Roundabout. It is The Fox and Hounds, and it is The Mawson Arms. There is a simple explanation. Originally there were two pubs side by side. One was owned by Fuller, Smith and Turner (their brewery is just behind the corner) and the other by another brewer. Fullers took over the second pub and combined the two into one pub. Regulars of each old pub didn't want to lose the identity of their local, so the brewers agreed to keep both names and have done so ever since.

would be liable. But when his own cows strayed, the lawyer said 'the case is altered'. Another explanation is that it comes from Casey's altar, a Catholic priest who had to say mass in secret (in places like sympathetic pubs) during the years of persecution. A third possibility is that a publican named his house after a favourite dancing spot in Spain, the Casa de Salter. Some say that it is a corruption of La Casa Alta, the house on the hill or the high house. There is, I feel, no definitive single answer to this sign.

Cat and Fiddle Again, there are varying stories. One says it comes from a French sign La Chatte Fidèle – the faithful cat. The more popular explanation

The Cat and Fiddle The pub name of the Cat and Fiddle was first recorded in the sixteenth century, earlier than these three sources. It probably came from an earlier, oral form of the nursery rhyme we know as 'Hey diddle diddle/The cat and the fiddle . . .' One earlier version started 'A cat came fiddling out of a barn . . .'

This old carved Cat and Fiddle is on the front of the Robinson's pub on the beautiful, wind-swept moors at Wildboarclough, near Macclesfield.

says it is from the old nursery rhyme, 'A cat came fiddling out of a barn, with a pair of bagpipes under her arm . . .'

Catherine's Wheel St Catherine of Alexandria was a fourth-century martyr. Of royal descent, she publicly admitted her Christianity and was put to death by torture on a wheel of sharp blades or spikes. According to legend, fire from heaven shattered the wheel spraying flames onto the onlookers whilst angels carried Catherine aloft. The Crusading Knights of St Catherine of Sinai took the Catherine Wheel as their badge. Catherine is also remembered by the wheel design in many church windows and the popular fireworks.

Chequers Pubs with many stories explaining their names can all be correct no matter which story they adopt for their particular pub. The Romans would emblazon a chequers sign on the outside of a Taberna to signify that games such as chess were played therein. The arms of the 'Great Earl Warenne' who was given the power of granting licences to sell beer are 'simply chequy or and azure'. During the middle ages a table divided into squares used by merchants of all sorts, accountants and judges to arrange matters of revenue was known as an exchequer.

The Chequers In this illustration of the Chequers pub name, the artists at Norman Hartley Signs have combined humour, modern history, tradition and, by implication, ancient history. In reverse order, the Chequers name's first roots were at Roman tabernae. The Romans used a chequerboard sign to indicate that board games, particularly a version of chess or draughts, could be played within. This was later strengthened as a pub name when the Earls of Warrenne were given the privilege and responsibility of licensing ale-houses in the Middle Ages and their coats of arms contained a chequered pattern. The building in the background is Chequers, the Prime Minister's residence and the reference to modern history.

The Chequers is a Mansfield pub in Pontefract, Yorkshire.

Cock and Bottle The cock appears on many pub signs because it is so easy to recognize and it often appears in combinations. The Cock and Bottle has at least three explanations. First, it represents a pub where you can get food, the cock, and drink, the bottle. A more popular explanation stems from the 'cock' being an old word for spigot or tap. Hence the meaning would be draught ale as well as bottled beverages. The third relates to the 'sport' of cock fighting. Since this often happened in and around pubs, some say this name is a more acceptable version of the Cock in Battle.

Crane While the Crane would seem to be a simple sign, meaning the bird, its use as a pub name sometimes has a different source. In centuries past, the crane was a device used to draw liquors from a cask.

Crooked Billet The origins of this name are obscure. Some say that a small log from which pub signs were made was called a crooked billet. Another theory relates it to a time when lots were drawn by pieces of stick, when it was desirable to get one without a crook, knot or other defect.

Crossed Keys This originated from the Papal Arms which typify St Peter. He was the accredited bearer of the keys of the Kingdom of God. The Apostle himself is sometimes shown, holding the keys.

Crossed Hands See Salutation

Crown There are more signs with this name than any other because the Crown is so frequently in combination with an Anchor, Sceptre, Cushion, Acorn, Ball, Barley Mow, Magpie, Three Sugar Loaves, etc. It might first have been used for pubs which were on Crown property but it is certainly a symbol of loyalty to and affection for the Monarch.

The Crown This photograph shows a pub sign which has been returned to the shop, worn at the edges. A duplicate sign was then painted by the Bowers brothers. The Crown has always been an extremely popular pub sign, alone or in combination with other objects. It portrays a loyalty to the crown and patriotism in a simple, quickly recognized pictorial.

The Crown is an Ind Coope pub at Anstey, Leics.

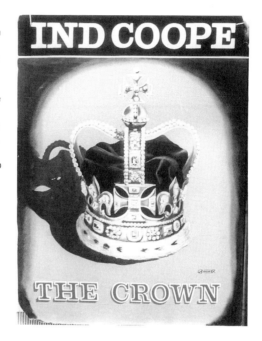

Crown and Thistle See Thistle and Crown

Dog On newer signs, a wide variety of dogs are depicted. The inspiration can come from the publicans, the customers, the brewery or a whim of the artist. But traditionally, dog signs were mostly the Talbot, for its heraldic connotations or a black dog. The Dog is a popular sign because it is a symbol of faithfulness, of being man's best friend. It is also the Christian symbol of the guardian guiding his flock. Animal signs have always been popular for several reasons. First, they were an intimate part of the lives of early settlers whose living came from the land. They were easy to depict and easy to recognize. And they frequently had heraldic connotations. So any particular animal sign could have a variety of reasons for being so named. In the eighteenth century, the Talbot pub in Over, Gloustershire was renamed the Dog in honour of the resident pet who tracked and helped catch some murderous thieves.

Dragon Like the Dog, the Dragon shares easy recognizability and heraldry.

The dragon is one of Britain's oldest heraldic charges. Before William the Conqueror it was the standard of the West Saxons. In the Bayeux tapestry a dragon on a pole is shown near King Harold. It was also a supporter on the arms of Henry VII and other Tudor sovereigns. There are Green Dragons, White Dragons and Red Dragons and the colour choice may have heraldic connections but equally well may be a traditional choice with the original reason for the colour choice lost in history.

Drunken Duck This is a pub named after an incident in its history. One day a publican's wife found her ducks lying dead outside the pub. Only when she began to prepare them for dinner did she discover that they were dead drunk but not dead. A leaking ale barrel had added beer to their feeding ditch.

Dun Cow Since dun is the name of a colour which is a mixture of brown and black, it would not appear to be a popular one to use on a pub sign. There is no one reliable source for this name. The dun cow is mentioned in twelfth-century Irish legend and Guy of Warwick is credited with slaying a savage beast, 'the dun cow'. But, more probably, some pubs were so named because of a dark cow living nearby.

Dusty Miller There is a pub sign outside Harlow, Essex which shows a fly fisherman in the background, casting, and a close-up of a fly called the Dusty Miller. This may confuse some people wondering about this name but the truth is much closer to what you would think if you just heard the name. The man who milled grain and corn was inevitably covered with dust and thus got his nickname, as did pubs near mills, especially in Yorkshire and Lancashire. The child's nursery rhyme also might have contributed to the sign, 'Millery, Millery, Dusty poll, How many sacks have you stole?'.

Dwarf There have been a few such pubs named after specific publicans or local characters. One such, the King's Porter and the Dwarf honoured Jeffrey Hudson. Hudson, who must have been a really *small* dwarf, lived and had many adventures in the 1600s. Once, at a party for the Queen given by Charles I, he was served up in a cold pie. On another gala occasion, he was drawn out of the pocket of William Evans, the huge door porter at the palace.

Eagle and Child This sign has a rather simple explanation but behind that connection lies a charming legend. The simple explanation is that it derives from the coat of arms of the Stanleys, Earls of Derby. In the time of Edward III (1327–77), a Sir Thomas Latham who was an ancestor of the Stanleys, is said to have had a child by a local woman. He directed the child be placed at the foot of a tree in which there was an eagle's nest. Taking a walk with his wife, he casually led her past the tree, pretended to find the infant and convinced her that they should adopt the child. A trusting wife is a treasure.

Eight Bells See Bells

Elephant and Castle A puzzling sign: why would, how could, an elephant carry a castle? The answer usually given is that it is a corruption of the title of the Portuguese wife of Charles II, the Infanta de Castile. But that is not correct, although it is a good story. It appeared as a carving on a bench in Ripon Cathedral in the late fifteenth century. It is said that elephants would carry men into battle in basket-like structures on their backs called 'castles'. The elephant and castle appears on several coats of arms, most notably the arms of the Cutlers' Company in 1622. Never willing to leave well enough alone, locals sometimes call these signs the pig and tinder box or pig and pepperbox!

Falcon While most pubs so named probably took the name because of the royal sport of falconry, this sign, too, has heraldic connections. It was a Yorkist sign and was the crest of Queen Elizabeth I. Falconry has also given us the sign of the Bird In Hand.

Feathers Tradition says that this sign, which is sometimes seen as the Prince of Wales's Feathers, Plume of Feathers, Prince's Arms and other names, comes from the Black Prince. In 1346 he defeated the King of Bohemia, John of Luxemburg and assumed his crest and motto, 'Hou Moet, Ich Dien' which was the subject of some controversy as to its meaning. Loosely translated, however, it apparently meant, 'keep courage, I am your companion in arms and I serve with you'. The Ich Dien and three ostrich plumes are still the crest of the Prince of Wales. This title derives from the time of Edward I who obtained the submission of Wales in 1284 and is conferred heir apparent to the throne. But calling it the Prince of Wales's feathers is a misnomer because it is the badge of the heir apparent whether or not he holds the title Prince of Wales. Some say it is a sign which came from poor painting and that it is really a debased version of a Fleur de Lys, the lilies of France.

Fighting Cocks Cock fighting was popular for centuries despite repeated attempts to curtail the 'sport'. Finally it was outlawed during the reign of Queen Victoria. Cock fights were frequently held at pubs and that led to the Fighting Cocks name as well as the Two Cocks, and some other names which were attempts to get away from the old image, as the Cock and Bottle.

First In, Last Out See Last

Fish This is a popular sign not just because of the sport and business of fishing but because the fish was originally a symbol of Christ. Three fishes is the symbol of the Holy Trinity.

Fish and Bell Fish are often combined on pub signs with other things such as the Crown, Case of Knives, Quart and Eels. The Fish and Bell could have been the result of two pubs merging but there is a much better story. A local lad who wasn't too bright would sometimes tie a bell around the neck of a fish he wanted to save for dinner or a future occasion. Then he would throw the fish back in the river, confident that he'd be able to find it again by listening for the bell.

Five Alls See Alls

Fleece Fleece was the source of England's wealth in the Middle Ages which is why the Chancellor sits on the woolsack. This sign is most frequently found in sheep farming and wool producing areas such as Yorkshire, or at a pub with an association with wool merchanting.

Fleur de Lys See Feathers

Fountain Many so-named pubs are at or near a source of good drinking water. The Fountain also has an obvious relationship with drinks of other kinds, as commemorated on a London pub sign 'Say what you will, when all is done or said, The best of drinking's at the Fountain Head'. But once again there is an earlier, religious and altogether more interesting source for this name. When St Paul was martyred it was by beheading. The legend says that his head, on being cut off, bounced three times and a fountain gushed up at each spot where his head landed. In Rome there is a Church of Three Fountains with an altar over each of the fountains. There is also a similar fountain connected with the martyrdom of St Alban, the first English martyr.

Four Alls See Alls

Fox While hundreds of signs of a straightforward sporting nature remember the fox alone or in combination with Hounds, Ducks or Rabbits, some signs have other meanings. The Intrepid Fox commemorates the eighteenth-century politician Charles James Fox and in Hertfordshire the Twin Foxes remembers local twin brothers who were notorious poachers. One Fox was altered to the Fox With His Teeth Drawn when the pub lost its seven-day licence.

Garland This sign usually shows a wreath or chaplet made of flowers, branches, feathers, ivy, etc. It is based on the time when a pub had to hang out an ale-garland to show it had just finished a new brew. The ale-conner, charged with the responsibility of checking ale and pubs for quality and measure in the Middle Ages, would then know to come and test the new brew.

Gay Dog Once called the Plough, the Gay Dog at Baughton, Worcester was renamed by the wife of the publican because he was such a 'gay old dog'. The pub sign shows a top-hatted white dog smoking a cigarette in a long holder.

George While today many of the pubs named the George show one of Britain's monarchs of that name on their pub sign, the original was named for St George of Dragon fame, hence the George and Dragon, St George and the Dragon and other combinations. Through the years some pubs have gone from the George to the George and Dragon and back again, making it very difficult to know why a particular pub is so named. St George has been adopted as the patron saint of England although little is known about him. The story of St George and the Dragon is thought to be an allegory for good against evil and has no basis in fact.

The Fox and Hounds As Fox and Hounds pub signs go, this is a pretty straightforward one. In this George Mackenney painting, the fox has obviously 'won', being across the river from the hounds. Perhaps because of the temper of the times, these signs are now mostly humorous, rather than showing the hounds (and hunters) winning. George has painted signs with the hound serving pints of beer to the foxes sitting at a pub table. He has also shown a smiling fox hiding in a tree while the hounds run past. There is a famous gallows sign stretching across the roadway at Barley, Herts, showing the hounds in perpetual pursuit of the fox.

The Fox and Hounds is a Mann pub in Stony Stratford.

George and Dragon See George

The George and Dragon In this fanciful version, George and the Dragon are getting set to share a pie and a pint. The sign is black and white and the words and figures are cut out in metal and fixed to the board. The pub itself is a sixteenth-century inn full of beams and history as well as an excellent collection of whisky water jugs, advertising memorabilia and old pub artifacts.

The George and Dragon is a Freehouse serving Marston's beers in Much Wenlock, Shropshire.

Globe It is a charge in heraldry and figures in the arms of the Clockmakers, Joiners and Spectacle Makers companies. The Globe was an emblem of Portugal and some British pubs took the name in order to advertise that wines of Portugal were to be had there.

Good Woman The Good Woman and the Silent Woman are usually depicted by a headless woman carrying her head underneath her arm. This

The Globe There are probably almost as many different reasons for calling a pub the Globe as there are pubs named the Globe, but the exact reason for this pub's name is not known. It used to be called Around the World and its

sign, usually meant humorously, comes from the tradition of beer being brewed and served by women, thus making them the butt of jokes and, sometimes, anger. But it also has quite another tradition which has been mostly forgotten. Martyrs who had been beheaded were usually depicted carrying their heads about for the benefit of believers. So early signs of this type undoubtedly referred to particular martyrs now impossible to identify but then became the 'joke' on women.

sign showed a globe with a man pushing through the top, a pint of beer in one hand and a loaf of bread in the other. Apparently man needed only those two things to get him through the world! The current sign is a tribute to man's first landing on the moon while the astronauts in their space vehicle return to a globe which is showing both the United States and the United Kingdom.

The Globe is a congenial McMullens pub in Codicote, Herts.

The Quiet Woman Some Quiet Woman signs include the couplet, 'Here is a woman who has lost her head. She's quiet now . . . you see, she's dead.' An earlier sign at this pub showed a ghostly headless woman with King Henry VIII in the background. This sign, painted by Paul Georgiou of Oldham Claudgen Ltd. includes the rhyme, 'Since the Woman is Quiet, Let no man breed a riot.' Local legend says an early publican had a nagging wife and chose the pub name as his revenge.

The Quiet Woman is an Ansell's pub in Leek, near Stoke on Trent.

Goat & Compass This pub name is probably a corruption of 'The Lord Encompasseth Us', a Puritan motto during the Commonwealth period. It is hard to say whether a Puritan or an enemy would apply the corrupted name to a pub.

Goat In Boots Another misunderstanding or mis-statement of phrase, this is believed to have started with a Chelsea pub called the Goat in the 1600s. Part of a Dutch legend said, 'Mercurius is der Goden Boode'. This means Mercury is the messenger of the gods and it was decided to make this the pub sign. Mercury went on one side and by accident or design Der Goden Boode became the Goat in Boots on the other.

Green Lettuce See Red Lattice

Green Man The Green Man is not really Robin Hood despite many present day signs. He was originally Jack o' the Green, a Celtic god and a medieval image of the spirit of fertility. He was sometimes called the Wild Man or the Wood Man. He dates from at least 1331 when Edward III gave a letter of protection to John Kempe of Flanders who began weaving cloth at Kendall in Westmorland. He produced a green cloth for foresters called Kendall Green. A similar but lighter green was made in Lincoln. Kendall Green and Lincoln Green became the cloths worn by woodmen, foresters, keepers, outlaws and verderers. The Green Man, with his resonances of fertility, was also a figure in May Day celebrations, wearing a green outfit covered with leaves.

Hand The Hand is usually combined with something else on pub signs, such as Gauntlet, Pen, Slipper or Bible. These would originally have been signs of some other trade where the Hand and another symbol would indicate the business. Either the premises became pubs or the tradesman changed his business and became a publican. In the seventeenth century, it was said that where a sign is painted with a woman's hand in it, 'tis a bawdy house' and where it has a man's hand it indicates another occupation.

Hand and Cock This is the kind of name whose meaning could easily be lost over time but, in this case, it is known to be a pun on the name of a one-time publican named Hancock.

Hand in Hand See Salutation

Hart Once again Christian symbolism appears to be the first reason for this sign. The Hart was the symbol for solitude and purity of life which certainly describes many pubs! The Hart is the male of the red deer. It is indigenous to Britain and is not an heraldic device. The White Hart is the one which appears on many arms and, because of that, on many pub signs.

Hedgehog Not a very popular sign now but one which used to show the Hedgehog with apples stuck to his quills. Early naturalists said the hedgehog would shake apples from a tree and then wallow in them, sticking them to his quills. Then he would go off to his hollow tree or other hole. But, if he should drop an apple when he was so loaded, he would throw down all the other apples in anger and go back for another load.

Highwayman Despite all the trouble they caused, highwaymen had close associations with pubs and many pubs are now named the Highwayman or by the name of a particular one. Dick Turpin, John Lyon, John Snooks and 16 String Jack have all been so honoured.

Hobson's Choice A pub name and sign honouring the man who gave rise to this phrase which many use without knowing why. A Cambridge publican named Tobias Hobson rented horses. But he insisted that the horses be taken out in strict rotation. He was so adamant about it that a Hobson's Choice came to mean no choice at all.

Hole in the Wall The choices here are: it comes from the Bible, Ezekiel, Chapter 8, verses 7–10 'and when I looked in behold a hole in the wall'. It was a hole in the wall of a debtor's prison through which the charitable could give the poor prisoners food, money or other donations. It comes from the practice of some pubs, particularly those on canal banks, to break a hole in the wall through which they could serve passers-by. It also referred to a snug or other small room in the pub which was reached through a small entrance, a hole in the wall. In the odd way of such things, the Hole in the Wall name has crossed the Atlantic. There is a refreshment room, a bar, in the House of Representatives in Washington, D.C. for the use of congressmen who call it the Hole in the Wall. There is a similar bar in the House of Commons for the use of MPs and their guests (not the general public) called the Strangers' Bar.

Honest Lawyer On these signs, lawyers receive the same treatment as women. The Honest Lawyer is normally shown as headless, with his head being under his arm or on a pile of law books. One nineteenth-century landlady in Southampton became disillusioned with the legal profession there and renamed her pub the Honest Lawyer where the sign shows the lawyer behind bars. On reflection, it is odd that not more professions have been given this treatment.

Hop Pole You might think that this would be an ancient subject for pub signs. Before the seventeenth century, what was then called ale was made from malt, yeast and water. It was strong and sweet and would not keep, despite many experiments and efforts. Then in the reign of William III the Dutch introduced hops to Britain and these were added to beer for flavouring and long life. It became known as hopping-beer. From that time, Hops and Hop Poles became the subjects of pub signs.

Hope The Anchor (see above) is the Christian symbol for hope. That sign led to the Hope and Anchor with 'hope' being shown as a woman in flowing robes. And that led to pubs simply called the Hope and, logically, their signs depict a woman in a flowing robe.

Intrepid Fox Generally this sign is said to honour Charles James Fox (1749–1806), the fearless politician who was known to have frequented the house in London's Wardour St. But another story is that the pub, which was called the Crown, changed its name in memory of an intrepid fox who took refuge there to avoid a hunt.

Jolly The Jolly Something signs began appearing in the eighteenth century and, if anything, are even more popular today. Seemingly every trade, work and many individuals have been so commemorated. There are Jolly Brewers, Sailors, Coopers, Farmers, Shiprights, Blacksmiths and so on. It is a good sign, reflecting as it does on the desired atmosphere of the pub.

Key London was late in calling 'keys' along the river 'quays', so some London pubs were named the Key. In other instances, it evolved from the locksmith trade, either by a pub moving to the premises or a locksmith changing profession.

King's Arms The King's Arms with its lion and unicorn has been a very

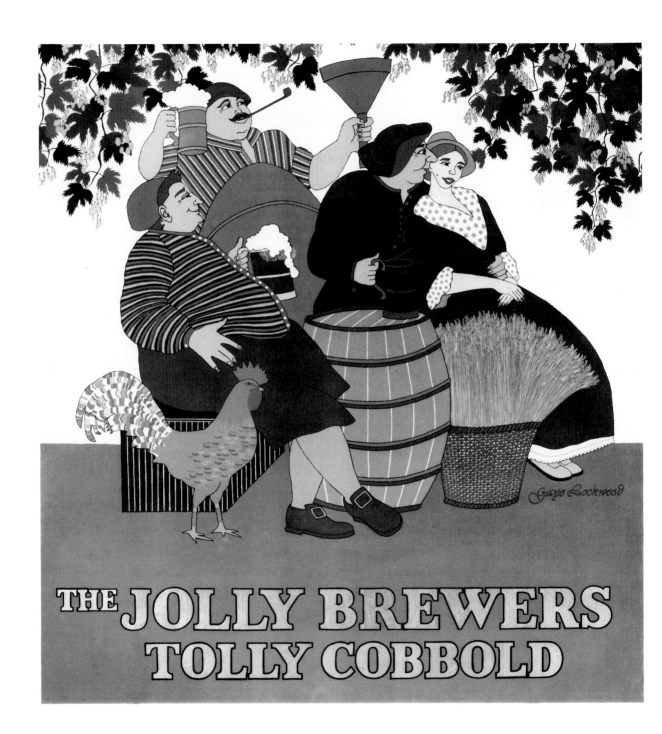

The Jolly Brewers The Jolly Someones is a jolly good name for a pub because a good pub visit should make you feel more jolly than before you went in. And, in olden days it means healthy and well-developed, another good association of ideas for a pub. In fact, adding 'jolly' to an otherwise straightforward name (the sailor, the butcher, etc.) instantly changes the image of the name and pub. Gaye Lockwood portrayed these elements on her very bold painting. The brewers are very healthy and well-developed and happy looking as are their customers.

The Jolly Brewers is a Tolly Cobbold pub in Milton, Cambridgeshire.

popular sign since James I (1603–25). Now a publican doesn't have to worry about his sign becoming politically unpopular and the need to hide or replace it. But that was not always so. During the Commonwealth, many such signs disappeared only to emerge with Charles II in 1660. Occasionally a sign takes a humorous approach and paints a king, usually Henry VIII, with a wench in his arms or using his arms and hands to hold certain parts of her anatomy.

King Charles in the Oak This sign, as does the more frequently seen Royal Oak, commemorates the future Charles II's escape from his enemies at Boscobel by hiding in an oak tree.

King's Head Like the King's Arms, this is a very popular sign for obvious reasons. King's Heads have been documented as early as 1446, that one being Henry VI of the House of York, but there were probably earlier ones. Of course, in those times there were also many Pope's Heads which were defensively changed to King's Heads with the Reformation. When the Princess (later Queen) Elizabeth was released from the Tower in 1558, she went first to the Church of All Hallows to give thanks and then to the King's Head in Fenchurch St to take refreshment.

King's Head and Good Woman The sign shows Henry VIII on one side and a headless Anne Boleyn on the other. It is quite a rare sign.

Labour in Vain The name is said to have originated in ballads about the ale-wives of England or Aesop's fables but the pictorial usually showed one or two women trying to scrub a black boy to make him white. In some cases, the reverse of the sign would show the woman standing with hands on hips looking perplexed.

The Labour In Vain Some signs include the rhyme, 'Washing here can now be seen. She scrubs both left and right. Although she'll get him middling clean, she'll never get him white'.

This Labour in Vain is a Bass Worthington pub in Yarnfield, near Stone, Staffordshire.

Lamb Originally this was meant to honour the Redeemer and it signifies meekness, purity, innocence and sacrifice.

Lamb and Anchor Following the meanings of the Lamb and the Anchor, this sign meant hope in God.

Lamb and Flag Again this is a religious relationship. This is known as the Agnus Dei or Lamb of God and represents Christ with the flag of his resurrection. It figures in the coat of arms of the Knights Templars and thus also has heraldic connections. It also figured in the arms of the House of Braganza and the crest of the Merchant Taylors.

Lame Dog This was a surprisingly popular sign in earlier centuries although a lame dog hardly seems a happy name for a pub! In one case, for a pub at Brierly Hill in the West Midlands, it was very appropriate. The pub was run by a collier who was lame because of an accident in the pits. The pub sign showed a lame dog trying to get over a stile and the inscription said, 'Stop,

A George Mackenney sketch depicting **The Lamb and Flag**.

my friends, and stay awhile, To help the Lame Dog over the stile'.

Last Not the last pub you'll see at the edge of a town, although this idea is sometimes expressed as the First In, Last Out. This sign and name usually honour the shoemaker because the last is the wooden form of a foot on which the shoes are formed. Perhaps publicans honoured this profession because of the proverb, 'Cobblers and tinkers are the best ale drinkers'.

Leather Bottle The makers of 'leathern botels' are mentioned as early as 1378 but legend says that the first leather bottle was seen by the passengers of Noah's Ark, floating on the flood. The leather bottle, actually much larger than usually shown on signs today, was the first known container for wine or beer.

Letters Today there is a Letters pub in Aspatria, Cumbria, whose sign shows an old lady reading a letter. In this case, local legend says that, in the days before most people could read, a scholar would visit the pub on scheduled days and read letters for the locals . . . for a fee, of course.

Lion Certainly a popular animal in pub terms. There are more lions shown on pub signs than any other animal. In fact, the Red Lion is the single most popular pub sign. Lions appear also as blue, black, gold, purple, brown, silver, white, yellow and green. Sometimes his colour depends on what paint is available so some pubs have changed the lion's colour from heraldic to realistic and back again at the whim of publican, artist or brewer. Some signs show single lions and others show several, again for no apparent reason. The red lion was the badge of John of Gaunt and lions have figured in the arms and badges of kings from the twelfth century.

The Red Lion Although there is no one listing of all licensed premises in the United Kingdom, the Red Lion is generally believed to be the most used pub sign. Counts vary between 800 and 1,100 Red Lions. It is also a very early pub sign. It is taken from the badge of John of Gaunt, Duke of Lancaster and fourth son of Edward III. He lived in the fourteenth century and the Red Lion appeared as a pub sign shortly after that. Normally the Red Lion is pictured as here, as the heraldic symbol. Occasionally it can be seen as a real lion, bathed red by a setting sun. This kind of heraldic red lion is sometimes called the 'ancient' red lion. This led to an amusing change in some pub names. In the late nineteenth century, when literacy was becoming widespread, many pubs proudly

changed to lettered signs. Some sign painters, daunted by the word 'ancient' used 'old' instead, leading pubs to be named the Old Red Lion even though there was no other one for comparison.

The Red Lion is a Benskins pub in Water End, Hemel Hempstead, Herts. It is a large, beamed pub dating from the 1600s and features a lovely, award-winning garden.

The Old Red Lion To an artist, a commission to paint a pictorial for the Red Lion or the Old Red Lion is not much of a challenge. There is no room for creativity when painting the heraldic symbol commonly used to illustrate this name. But, in this case, George Mackenney was asked for a fresh approach. This is his sketch for the Old Red Lion which has since been approved and painted.

Lion and Castle This sign originated in the arms of the royal family of Castile and originally advertised that wine from Spain was available in the pub.

Lion and Lamb In Christian symbolism the lion is the emblem of the resurrection and the lamb is the symbol of the Redeemer and together they represent the millennium, the lion lying down with the lamb.

Little Devil The Devil is not the most popular character on pub signs but this pub which existed in London at the beginning of the 1700s inspired a lovely description of a barmaid. Ned Ward described her as, 'tolerably handsome, who can laugh, cry, say her prayers, sing a song, all in a breath, and can turn in a minute to all sublunary points of a female compass'.

Live and Let Live The most probable story for this name came from the days when churches, notably the Methodists, would try to get pubs closed so that people wouldn't drink. Nearby pub owners were likely to say, 'We've been here longer. Why can't they live and let live?' A more fanciful version says that it relates to St George. After he slew the dragon, a maiden was praising him and she suddenly saw a worm. She implored St George to kill it. But he replied that as the worm was harmless, he'd rather Live and Let Live.

Lunways Another example of a pub with a name based on local tradition and lore. Lunways, in Micheldever, Hampshire, was founded in 1470 as the Lundun Ways. Long before railroads or even stagecoaches, this was a drover's inn, the place where the drovers gathered to drive their cattle, sheep and other animals to east and west 'Lundun' for sale.

Lute & Tun This sign, showing a lute and a large cask of beer or ale, is one of the pun signs.
In this case, Lute and Tun = Luton in Bedfordshire.

Mad Cat and **Mad Dog** Actually the Mad Dog pub came first. A publican decided that his favourite customers were 'mad dogs', ones who have a great horror of water! Not to be outdone, a nearby pub named itself the Mad Cat.

Magpie A most peculiar bird, being thought by some to be a bird of good omen and by others to bring ill luck, its original name was the pie. For its antics, it was given the nickname 'maggoty' and maggoty + pie eventually became Magpie. A nursery rhyme goes 'Round about, Round about, Maggoty Pie, My father loves good ale and so do I'. So some early pubs had the rather unappetizing name of the Maggoty Pie! The bird is regarded as uncanny. It is often shown in combination with Stump or Crown or Platter.

Man in the Moon While today this will as often as not feature Neil Armstrong, the first astronaut to set foot on the moon, it is a very old sign. Pubs chose the name because of legends, fables and writings of Shakespeare and Chaucer. The traditional sign shows a half moon and the man carries a bundle of sticks and a lantern and leads a dog.

Marquis of Granby While this listing of pub signs has ignored individuals because it is normally obvious why they are honoured by the sign, the Marquis of Granby is different. For one thing, you see pubs with this name all over Britain. The Marquis of Granby, John Manners (1721–1770), was a colonel in the royal regiment of Horse Guards and he was regarded as the soldiers' friend. He would finance wounded ex-soldiers and help them set up in business, usually as publicans. So he is remembered both for valour and charity.

Maypole May Day in England used to be dedicated to Robin Hood and Maid Marian because Robin died on that day. Maypoles were erected in villages and people enjoyed a day of dancing, feasting, archery and other sports and activities, sometimes to the detriment of virtue. Naturally, pubs at or near the site of the maypole took that happy name.

Mitre The Mitre is a head-dress worn by bishops and cardinals. It derives from the Greek, *mitra*, for headband. In a kind of reverse logic, this became a popular name for a pub after the Reformation if the pub was on the site which formerly had religious uses. It is, however, even older as a pub sign, being first noted in 1460.

Mitre in the Hoop In ancient times, many pub signs were carved representations hung inside a hoop. Thus the pub often became known as the Mitre (or Hart or Grapes or Swan or Cock) in the Hoop. The hoop was often made to represent a bush or covered with evergreens. Versions of these signs continued until at least the beginning of the eighteenth century.

Mother Huff Cap A sign of uncertain origin, it is often confused with Mother Red Cap (below) and perhaps they come from the same source. Both have been seen since the 1600s. Huff-cap is the old term for the froth or head on a jug of beer. The only way the drinker could judge the beer, because it was served in solid vessels, was by the amount and colour of the huff-cap.

Mother Red Cap The precise identity of this person is now obscure. She could come from Skelton's alewife Elynour Rummyng. Or she was an old nurse at Hungerford Stairs. Or she was Moll Cutpurse, the female highway robber of the 1650s, who had connections with Camden Town's Mother Red Cap pub. Finally, of course, she could be Mother Huff Cap, which brings us full circle.

Mother Shipton At least we know who she was! Mother Shipton was a prophet in Yorkshire, said to have lived from 1488–1561. Her predictions and prophecies have been in print since 1641.

Mug House Originally the Mug House Club in London's Long Acre in the early eighteenth century. There were about a hundred members who met every Wednesday and Saturday. They were lawyers, gentlemen and tradesmen. Each had his own separate mug and nothing was drunk but ale. A harpist played all evening and from time to time a member would rise and entertain with a song. There was no room for any subject like politics which might sour conversation.

Nag's Head As a pub sign, this appears to be a corruption of the Horshed and Horshead which were pub names. The Nag's Head is also a modern day 'humorous' sign. On one side it shows a horse's head and on the other a nagging woman's head, a spiritual relative of the Good Woman and Silent Woman.

New Inn There are two main reasons for a pub to have this name. First, because it is a new pub, newer than the others nearby. The other and more interesting source dates to the time of Queen Elizabeth I. That Monarch travelled the land to demonstrate that peace and prosperity had arrived and was bothered by the scarcity and condition of the inns. She directed that new inns be built for the benefit of travellers.

Noah's Ark This could be a sarcastic reference to the mixed crowd of characters one finds in a pub. More likely it was inspired by the biblical story and because it is from the arms of the Shipwright's Company. The Shipwright's motto might also have a certain appeal for publicans adopting this sign: Within The Ark, Safe For Ever.

Oak The oak, an emblem of Britain, is popular as a pub sign. Certainly the Royal Oak commemorating the escape of King Charles II is frequently seen. This tree is also seen as simply the Oak or the British Oak, in combination with something else as in the Oak and Ivy or commemorating a particular tree, as in the Saling Oak in Essex.

Odd One Out Possibly the only pub with this odd name is in Colchester. It was once the Mermaid, a theatrical pub visited by Houdini and Charlie Chaplin. The pub was closed for eleven months a few years ago and then sold as a freehouse. The new owner decided to feature a variety of real ales, very unusual at the time, and the pub was thought to be the Odd One Out of all the pubs in town.

Old, Olde, Ye Olde A great number of pub signs in this listing probably appear somewhere preceded by Old, Olde, Ye Olde or New or Young! These are generally ignored here as they only confuse the basic stories of the names. Obviously these adjectives are mostly used to distinguish a pub from a nearby one with the same name (in this regard, see Pretty Bricks below) or to emphasize a pub's age or antiquity. Having said that, several listings properly start with 'old'.

Old English Gentleman Not seen much anymore, this and the John Bull, Ancient Briton, True Briton, Generous Briton all represented the notion of Great Britain at its finest.

Old Red Lion Towards the end of the last century when literacy was becoming very common, there was a tendency to get away from pictorial pub signs and celebrate the fact that people could read lettered signs without the help of a picture! Since the heraldic red lion is known as the ancient red lion, that should have been put on an all lettered sign. But owing to poor spelling, laziness or speed, some became the Old Red Lion.

Old Parr's Head Named quite properly after Thomas Parr who was born in 1483. He lived to be 152 and is credited with having an illegitimate child when he was over 100 and, having married his second wife Catherine Milton when he was 120, had another child with her.

Our Lady Our Lady and the Virgin, both names for Mary, the Mother of God, were popular before the Reformation. In those days, public houses were honouring saints and calling on them for protection.

Palm Tree As a symbol, the Palm Tree is much older than most. It was said to be a strong image of the early Christians – rough and rugged below but increasing in beauty upwards where it bears heavenly fruit.

Paviours Arms As a pub sign this is only a couple of centuries old, stemming from the time when publicans and artists began dignifying trades by displaying their unofficial 'arms'. That was also the time of a growing demand for pavers to improve the condition of city streets.

Peacock The peacock appeared in ancient mythology and was shown on Roman coins. The supposed incorruptibility of its flesh led to it representing the Resurrection and caused people to take oaths 'by the Peacock', oaths that were always kept.

Pelican Strange as it seems, this ungainly bird was once a symbol for Christ.

Dante called Christ 'our pelican'. It was also a symbol of charity but there are those who say that pubs are so named because of their enormous bills.

Peter and Paul This sign had a good story as to its origin but, unfortunately, it isn't true. The story says that the sign originated in London where there was a St Peter's church – Westminster Abbey – and, of course, St Paul's. St Paul's was in need of repairs and many of the estates of St Peter's were appropriated to pay for the repairs, thus 'robbing Peter to pay Paul'. It sounds good but the phrase has been noted as far back as the fourteenth century and may well have no more complex origin than being the names of two of Christ's greatest followers.

Pickled Egg Many pubs have royal connections which are usually good for business. This sign originated when Charles II stopped to eat at a pub in Clerkenwell in London and, for the first time, had some pickled eggs. The landlord was so flattered that he adopted the name and sign of the Pickled Egg.

Piddle Inn Seems an altogether appropriate name for a pub! The Piddle is a river in Piddletrenthide, Dorset and the pub was named after the river. The sign shows a worried farmer floating on the river in a chamber pot.

Pied Pied animals appear on a variety of pub signs such as the Pied Bull, Ox, Dog, Calf, Cow, Horse and Leopard. Pied means variegated or spotted and has a relationship with spotted animal signs. Pied, and Piebald, probably derive from Magpie (which comes from pie and maggoty-pie) and bald 'streaked with white' as on Bald-faced Stags.

Pig and Tinderbox Never ones to leave an already odd name well enough alone, pubgoers sometimes call the Elephant and Castle the Pig and Tinderbox. Similarly, Crown and Sceptres are sometimes called Hat and Snake.

Pig and Whistle Usually a humorous sign showing a standing pig playing on a whistle, the only agreement about the origin is that it is very old. To start with the religious, it could be a corruption of the angel greeting Mary with *Pige Washael* or Health to the Maiden. There is general agreement that the whistle comes from *washael* or good health. But pig could come from the time when beer was served in pails, into which you'd dip your mug or horn, your 'pig'. Or pig could come from the practice of having pegs inside large tankards, each peg being a half-pint. As the tankard was passed around, each drinker took his peg. If someone offended his fellows, he was 'taken down a peg or two' meaning he lost his round. Finally, *piggin* is an old English name for a wooden vessel with a handle.

Plough This name and sign has very obvious agricultural meanings and relationships. It is a very old sign, originally found on pubs in farming areas which, of course, meant almost the whole country. Sometimes the Plough sign will show the constellation Ursa Major. In the middle ages, ploughs were blessed shortly after Christmas and a decorated plough was used to raise

The Pretty Bricks If your pub is named the New Inn and two other pubs named the New Inn are opened nearby, what would you do? That happened to this seventeenth-century pub about 100 years ago. Actually, they didn't have to do anything but let the locals continue to call it what they were calling it anyway: the Pretty Bricks, referring to the painted brickwork on the front of the pub. So, to this day, the pub continues to have an official name, the New Inn, the formal name it is known as, the Pretty Bricks, and the name most of today's regulars call it, simply the Bricks.

The Pretty Bricks is an Ansells pub on John St. in Walsall, near Birmingham.

plough-money to make a special plough-ale.

Plume of Feathers See Feathers

Poet's Head Usually a sign to commemorate some famous poet. But one such Poet's Head was the result of a king's death. When Charles I was beheaded, Taylor, the water poet, put the sign of the Mourning Bush up at his London tavern to express his grief. When he was forced to take that down, he put up his own portrait with the words, 'There is many a head hangs for a sign; Then, gentle reader, why not mine'. Thus, the Poet's head, was a political statement.

Pope's Head See Bishop's Head

Pretty Bricks In the nineteenth century, when two more pubs were built in the town of Walsall and both were called the New Inn, it became difficult to know which pub you were talking about. So the locals of the oldest New Inn began calling it the Pretty Bricks, describing the painted brick front of the pub. Pub regulars are always ready to supply nicknames and sometimes they become official.

Prince of Wales' Feathers See Feathers

Prince's Arms See Feathers

Punch Bowl Strange as it may seem, this was originally a political sign, or at least had political connections. It is named after the drink which became popular at the end of the seventeenth century. Punch was the fashionable drink and became the drink of the Whigs and was served at taverns they frequented. Tories drank claret, sack and canary which reminded them of times past. The Punchbowl was also connected on signs with other Whig symbols, thus the Punchbowl and Crown, the Magpie and Punchbowl and the Union Flag and Punchbowl.

Q Through the centuries there have been pubs known only by a letter or a series of letters (see Letters) with their meaning unknown or obscure. Being different, they are certainly eye-catching. There is a Q at Stalybridge in Cheshire.

Quart Pot See Tankard

Queen's Arms Pubs bearing the Queen's arms multiplied with the popularity of 'good Queen Bess', Queen Elizabeth I, and even today, many so-named pubs still carry her coat of arms. In a broader sense, this is another sign expressing affection and loyalty for the Crown. In that regard, it doesn't matter which Queen's arms are displayed and, indeed, they sometimes change with the painting of a new sign.

Queen's Head Again this sign gained popularity because of the beloved Queen Elizabeth I but it appeared before her day. In fact, it probably first

The Queen's Head This beautiful portrait is of one of the two most popular Queens to appear on these signs, Queen Elizabeth I. The other was Queen Victoria.

The Queen's Head is an Ind Coope pub in Wisbech, Cambridgeshire and the painting is by Malcolm Bowers.

The Barbridge The Barbridge is a canal side pub, taking its name from a nearby bridge over the canal. So what is more appropriate than a pub sign imitating the restful scene. Miles Arrindell, in one of his few full-size pub signs, painted this for one of his favourite pubs near his home.

The Barbridge Inn is a Boddingtons pub on the Grand Union canal on Chester Road outside Nantwich, Cheshire.

The Cross Keys In Christian iconography, crossed keys are a symbol of St. Peter because it was Peter to whom Jesus gave the keys to the kingdom of Heaven. The papal arms have shown the crossed keys, and they also appear in the arms of a number of bishops, such as those in Gloucester, Ripon and Exeter. In this portrait sign by George Mackenney, you wonder what St. Peter is thinking as he contemplates the book of applicants to The Heaven which he guards.

The Britannia, one of the most traditional signs, for obvious reasons.

The Cloggers Arms Where else but Lancashire would you find the Cloggers Arms? Ron Kitchen, painting an assignment for Butterfield Signs, created this warming portrait of a clogger at work. Such is an artist's skill that you feel you want to know this craftsman. Artisans' arms and tradesmen's arms vary between literally showing a coat of arms and, as in this instance, showing the workman using his arms (not to mention his hands) to produce his wares.

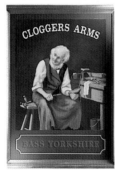

The Cloggers Arms is a Bass pub in Oldham, Lancashire.

The Cramond Inn The Cramond Inn dates from the sixteenth century and is located where the Romans built a fort and a port. From this point they are said to have circumnavigated the British Isles. The pub sign shows General Agricola with one of his sailing ships in the background. Whenever the pub tries to build an addition or expand parking, work is slow while Roman artifacts are dug up and studied. This warm and friendly pub was once a haunt of Robert Lewis Stevenson. Scenes in his books, while they have different names, are clearly of this area.

The Cramond Inn is a freehouse in Cramond, Edinburgh, Scotland. The pub sign was painted by Kirkland Main, Dean of the Faculty of Art at the Edinburgh College of Art. He was asked to paint the sign by his wife who cooks at the pub and whose father used to be the publican there.

The Elephant and Castle This Elephant and Castle is an Eldridge Pope pub in West Moors, Dorset. The sign was painted by Brewery Artists.

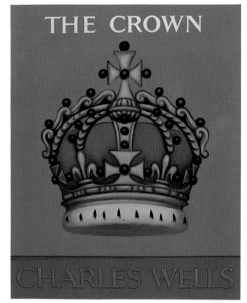

Immediate humour is shown in this particularly impressive sign for **The End of the World.**

The Endeavour This sign has two sides, as one of the pub's regulars suggested two famous Endeavours be pictured and a young, local graduate artist named Stan Corkhill was commissioned. One side depicts the Endeavour of Captain Cook which went on the first voyage of discovery to Australia. The other side, painted mostly in black and white to reflect the lack of colour in outer space, shows the American Apollo 15 spaceship. It was called the Endeavour because its 1971 mission came just two hundred years after Cook's mission.

The Endeavour is on the Springfield Road in Chelmsford, Essex.

The Crown, another extremely widespread name.

The Fleece Butterfield Signs in Bradford, West Yorkshire is a sixty-one year old firm of commercial sign manufacturers. One fine artist subcontracting for Butterfield, Ron Kitchen, painted this lovely pictorial of The Fleece. He took a realistic, descriptive approach to the subject, showing the sheep being shorn of his fleece. Many Fleece signs relate the product to its importance to Britain when its fortunes rested on the wool produced.

The Fleece is a Bass pub in Mossley, Greater Manchester.

The Jolly Cobblers

The Green Man, the sign that lends itself to both simple and elaborate designs.

The Three Horseshoes is usually given a straightforward heraldic treatment. Here, a charming blacksmiths scene has been chosen instead.

The Goat in Boots is a corruption of the Dutch phrase 'Mercurius is der Godan Boode', which means 'Mercury is the messenger of the Gods'.

The Merchant LFA Ltd of Lancaster decided to pay homage to both William Younger, founder of the brewery which is now part of Scottish and Newcastle, and Hans Holbein the artist. The Merchant as a pub name goes back at least to the days of the Company of Merchant Taylors who made linings for suits of armour and men's clothing. Later guild members became general merchants and that category would certainly include publicans.

The Merchant is a Wm.

Youngers pub in Lancaster which was established in 1688. The painting is by Frank Perkins of LFA.

The Martyrs This pub is located in Tolpuddle and the martyrs here were the six farm labourers who, in 1833, formed a union to resist the cut in their wages from nine shillings to eight. They were arrested, tried and convicted under the Mutiny Act of 1797 and sentenced to be sent to Australia for 7 years. In 1836, after a public outcry, they were pardoned. Their ordeal helped establish trades unions in Great Britain. The quote is from John Ball's text for a sermon at the outbreak of the Peasant's Revolt, adapted from a poem by Richard Rolle of Hampole, 'When Adam delved and Eve span,

Who was then the gentleman?'.

The Martyrs is a Hall and Woodhouse pub in Tolpuddle, Dorset. The memorable sign was painted by the brewery artist John Hawkins.

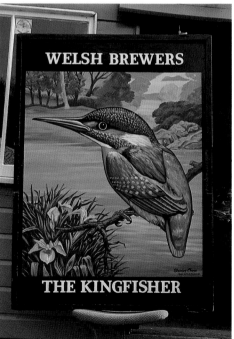

The Letters This painting expresses the feelings which are evident in the story of the pub name yet does not accurately portray that story. As well as can be determined from local legend, the pub's name came from the illiteracy of people in the last century. The local pub, being so important as the social centre in the community, was where people came when they received letters they could not read. The practice developed that a scholar would regularly visit the pub and, for a small fee, read the letter to the recipient and write a reply.

The Letters is a Jennings Brewery pub in Aspatria, Cumbria. The sign is by Franklin Advertising of Liverpool.

The Kingfisher The relatively few pubs with this name are normally found near rivers or canals. Stanley Chew painted this lovely portrait of the bird. There are thought to be about ninety different kinds of birds shown on pub signs, usually because they appear in the area or because some publican had a fondness for a particular kind of bird. Ordinary birds are depicted, birds like the crow, the robin, the blue tit, the jay and more unusual birds like the pelican.

The Kingfisher is a Welsh Brewers (a part of Whitbread) pub in Cymbran, Wales.

The Ring O' Bells When you see a pub named the Bell or the Six Bells (or some other number of bells) you can be reasonably sure that there is a church nearby. The number of bells on a pub sign may not have any specific meaning but eight bells is the usual number of peals. The Ring O' Bells is often found on a pub where the bell ringers gather after their efforts.

This Ring O' Bells was painted by Frank Perkins of LFA Ltd. and shows five hand bell ringers wearing the clothing of their full time occupations. They appear to be making their music outside the pub.

The Ring O' Bells is a Mitchell's pub in Lancaster.

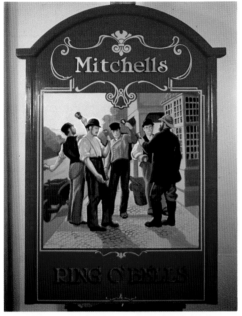

The Oarsman This pub's sign is on the ground level and is about six feet high by four feet wide. It is a dramatic painting of the survivors of a naval battle rowing for their lives. It's also a good example of how a name and sign change can change the personality of a pub. This pub used to be called the Oxford and Cambridge and celebrated the annual race between the two universities. Now the refurbished pub has a generally nautical decor but is no longer specific to that boat race.

The Oarsman is a Wm. Younger pub just off High Holborn in London.

The Old Royal Ship While there is no known reason why this particular pub came to be called The Old Royal Ship, it is a variation on a very frequently-seen pub name and sign. This eliptical sign is based on Payne's accurate engraving of The Sovereign of the Seas. She proudly flies the Royal Banner and the flag of the Lord High Admiral, announcing that both the Sovereign and the Admiral were on board. The jack on the bows is the newly formed combination of the crosses of Saints George and Andrew following the union of the Crowns.

The Old Royal Ship is a Whitbread pub in Luckington, Wiltshire. The pictorial was painted by Brewery Artists.

The Royal George, a fine naval sign commemorating a warship.

The Robin Hood Robin is a very popular pub sign subject, just as he is popular in legend. This Robin Hood was painted by Malcolm Bowers for the Ind Coope pub of that name in Bramshell, Derbyshire in 1973 and has since been redone because, like all pub signs, weathering and pollution take their toll.

The Shakespeare's Head In this carved pub sign, supplemented by a nearby painted board, William Shakespeare looks down benevolently on the doings in London's Carnaby Street. The pub was established here about 1735 when this was the centre of an eighteenth century market. It was founded by two distant relatives of the poet, Thomas and John Shakespeare. The carved Shakespeare's Head survived World War II except for its right hand, which was blown off when a bomb landed nearby during the Blitz.

The Shakespeare's Head is a Watney's pub on London's Great Marlborough Street.

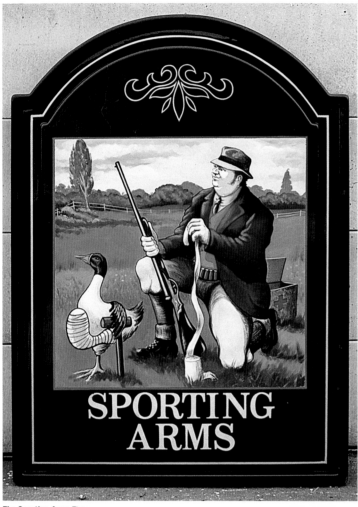

The Sporting Arms There are two kinds of pub signs and names connected with sports. In this case, Norman Hartley Signs took a light hearted approach. They portrayed a true sportsman – a hunter but willing to patch up the wounded!

The Sporting Arms is a Cameron's pub in Blaydon, Tyne and Wear.

A particularly elegant interpretation of **The Sugar Loaf**, showing a landscape based on the mountains around Rio de Janeiro.

referred to Mary, the Queen of Heaven. Now, many Queens are so honoured but since the Queen is rarely mentioned by name on the sign, we have to depend on the artist's skill and accuracy to be sure which Queen it is. In 1636 John Taylor wrote:

> 'These Queenes heads like the Kings heads are, I see,
> Both are one sex, both wood, both paintings be:
> There is but little difference in the Signes
> And sure there is small odds amongst their Wines.'

Quiet Woman This is a variation of the Good Woman (see above) but the landlady of a Queen's Head in 1745 illustrates why such pubs came about. The woman, of the Queen's Head in Kingston, Surrey was ordered by the court to be ducked for scolding! She was placed in a chair and ducked in the river Thames in the presence of 2000–3000 people. Either she was popular or she had scolded a lot of people who couldn't wait to see her ducked.

Railway With the coming of railroads in the first half of the last century, the coaching inns began their inevitable decline, to be replaced by railway pubs. These were built at locations where there were passengers getting on and off trains and where there were railway workers. Such pubs were named after viaducts, tunnels, coats of arms of the rail companies, bells, views and so on. Others were named after particular trains or engines.

Ram While sheep seldom make an appearance on signs, rams are popular. They can be chosen for a pub name for a number of reasons, the most obvious has to do with the wool trade. But the Ram is also a sign of the Zodiac and this has led to some instances of use. The ram is also an heraldic animal, usually with golden horns and hoofs and he appears on the arms of the Clothworkers, Drapers and Leathersellers Companies.

Raven The Raven and the Black Raven are popular pub signs despite that bird's reputation for representing bad luck. In Christian art, the bird is an emblem of God's caring for his subjects; it was a raven which brought food to Elijah. The Raven was the badge of the old Scottish kings and a Jacobite symbol and this would cause some pubs of supporters to be so named.

Red Lattice In earlier centuries, as indeed today, the ideal pub allows its customers to see what is going on outside the pub without passers-by being able to see clearly into the pub. Thus the privacy of the patrons was assured. Today pubs do it with carefully placed windows, coloured glass, curtains and wavy glass. The same was once achieved by putting latticework over windows and the lattice was traditionally painted red or green. And, in the way of these things, this led to pubs being named after their prominent feature – the Red Lattice and the Green Lattice and, as these names became corrupted, the Lettuce. Today there is a group of pubs in and around London named the Slug and Lettuce and this probably has no relationship to the Lattice, but is, rather, a memorable combination.

Red Lion The Red Lion is the badge of John of Gaunt, Duke of Lancaster, the fourth son of Edward III. He lived from 1340–1399 and the Red Lion began appearing as a pub sign during the following century. The Red Lion of Scotland is quartered on the shield of Britain and is there shown as a red lion rampant on a gold field. It is normally shown as the heraldic red lion on a plain background but is occasionally depicted as a real lion or humorously.

Red, White and Blue Not, as you might suppose, a reference to the Union Jack or the flag of the United States, this came from an old sea song as did the sign of the Three Admirals.

Ring O'Bells See Bells

Rising Sun The rising sun is a natural for a pub sign as it symbolizes a new start, a beginning day or business or pleasure. Throughout history, the rising sun symbolized beginnings and a setting sun, the end. It also appears in heraldry as the badge of Edward III, a crest of the Distiller's Company and forms part of the arms of Ireland. It is sometimes painted humorously as a sun with a human face, yawning and stretching.

Robin Hood This is probably the most frequent of signs coming from ballads. It is sometimes Robin Hood alone and other times with Little John. Robin Hood is generally believed to be legend, perhaps a last remnant of the Saxons. If some legends are taken literally, he was born in 1160 and didn't die until 1325! His good humour and daring help disguise his habit of taking things which didn't belong to him. Some pubs accompany their signs with this inscription or variations of it:
    'You gentlemen and yeomen good,
    Come in and drink with Robin Hood.
    If Robin Hood be not at home,
    Come in and drink with Little John.'
One country publican, more interested in accuracy and his own name than in poetry, changed the last line to: 'Come in and drink with Jimmy Webster'.

Rose The reasons for the use of the Rose as a pub sign would vary depending on when the pub was established. Originally, the Rose was a symbol of the Virgin Mary and as such would have been popular in early centuries. Then came the Golden Rose, the badge of Edward I (1272–1307). Then came the Red Rose of Lancaster and the White Rose of York and the War of the Roses. After the union of the disputants, the Tudor Rose became the badge of the House of Tudor and the national emblem. Today roses are painted all colours, not necessarily tying any particular rose to any bit of history or heraldry. The Rose is also frequently combined with other things on signs, most notably the Rose and Crown. The Rose and Thistle symbolizes the union of England and Scotland.

Rose and Crown When the marriage of Henry VII and Elizabeth of York ended the feudal battling between the houses of York and Lancaster, the Tudor Rose, half red and half white, surmounted by the crown became the royal badge. This Rose and Crown led to the popularity of this pub sign although today it is seen in all sorts of pictorials, not necessarily true to the Tudor Rose.

The Yorkshire Rose For this pub sign, Ron Kitchen for Butterfield Signs took a very traditional approach in the style of the painting, but a very untraditional one in the content. Most pubs with a rose in the name show a painting of a rose on the sign. Ron chose to depict Elizabeth of York as the Yorkshire Rose . . . but, for good measure, she is holding a white rose of Yorkshire. With Elizabeth's marriage to Henry VII, the roses of Yorkshire and Lancaster became one in the Tudor Rose, so often found on Rose and Crown pub signs.

The Yorkshire is a Bass Yorkshire pub in Guiseley, West Yorkshire.

Rose Revived This became a popular pub name and sign with the restoration of Charles II although not every pub of this name honours that event. There was a pub in Newbridge, Oxon called the Rose which had to be moved to a new site across the river. Once this was successfully accomplished it became known as the Rose Revived and its sign showed a rose floating in a mug of beer.

The Royal Oak Artists have a wide choice when it comes to portraying this popular pub name. Some do a straightforward 'portrait' of the tree itself, many do the tree with a crown superimposed on it, others show the tree with the face of Charles II on it, others show soldiers hunting below whilst we can see Charles II hiding in the tree. Other variations are the medal struck to commemorate the event and one of the ships bearing the name. Here artist Eileen Wood tells the story without showing Charles II at all, just a Roundhead looking for him in vain.

The Royal Oak is a Bass Yorkshire pub in Holmfirth, Yorkshire.

Royal Oak After the battle of Worcester in 1651, Charles II escaped by concealing himself in an oak tree at Boscobel. An enactment in 1664 established Royal Oak Day on the King's birthday, 29 May, and this was celebrated for centuries. The popularity of this pub sign, and the similar King Charles in the Oak, is mostly because it shows loyalty and affection for the Crown but also because it is such a good story! The signs show a crown superimposed on an oak tree, the King's face on the tree, a figure of the King, straight or comical, sitting in the tree or, occasionally, just the tree.

Running Footman In the eighteenth century, wealthy families employed running footmen. It was their job to run in front of the carriage, clearing the path, bearing torches at night, paying tolls and otherwise serving the carriage passengers. Whenever the Duke of Queensbury wanted to hire a new running footman, he would have the candidate put on the Duke's fancy livery and run past his balcony along Piccadilly. One such candidate

I Am The Only Running Footman The Running Footman, as it is more frequently called these days, is still going strong in London's Mayfair. In the eighteenth century, wealthy families employed running footmen to run ahead of their carriages. The footmen cleared the path, paid tolls, carried torches at night and, in any other way required, served the passengers. As far as is known, the pub name is quite correct today, it is the only one so named. This engraving of the pub sign is from *Old and New London* circa 1880. It is another opportunity to observe that pub signs have changed little over the centuries.

presented himself under the balcony after his trial run. The Duke said 'That will do, you suit me well'. To this the man replied, 'Your livery suits me well', ran off and was never seen again. A pub in London's Mayfair correctly proclaims the present-day truth on its sign, I Am the Only Running Footman.

Running Man Outside London, the Running Man occasionally survives on signs as a remnant of the Running Footman.

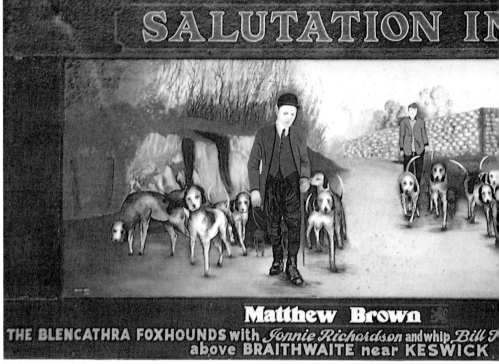

St George and the Dragon Did St George ever really exist? Or is his
legendary battle with the dragon a corruption of St Michael conquering the
Devil? Whatever the truth, St George and the Dragon makes a very colourful
sign and remains popular today under that name and also as the George.
After all, in the words of a seventeenth-century rhyme:

    'To save a mayd St George the dragon slew –
    A pretty tale if all is told be true.
    Most say there are no dragons, and 'tis said,
    There was no George; pray God there was a mayd'.

St John's Head Worth mentioning is a pub sign which appears in one of
Hogarth's pictures. It shows the head of St John the Baptist on a charger.
Underneath is the pub's announcement, 'Good Eating'!

Salutation This is another instance of a name changing its meaning, as
represented by the pub sign, over the centuries. For early pubs the Salutation
meant the Angel Gabriel saluting the Virgin Mary. With the coming of the
Reformation and the decline of religious signs, the image shown became a
soldier and citizen greeting each other. This in turn led to two citizens
bowing to each other and then to today's version of two hands conjoined. It
is also sometimes known as Hand in Hand and possibly led to the Crossed
Hands.

Above. A brilliant depiction of
The Salutation for a pub in
Cumbria. Right. A Mackenney
treatment for a Ship
commission.

134

Same Yet As in the story of George Mackenney and the Oat Sheaf (Chapter 4), you have to be careful what you say to the artist. Some time ago, the Seven Stars at Prestwich had to have its weathered sign repainted. When the artist asked the publican what to put on the signboard, the publican replied, 'the same yet'. The artist took him at his word and that's become the name of the pub.

Saracen's Head Saracen is a convenient name to describe any non-European. When Englishmen came home from fighting the Saracens, the villains were pictured as being huge with terrible faces, thus making the tales of battle more impressive. After the Crusades, many knights added a Turks head to their armorial bearings. That is why today the Saracen's head is usually depicted as vicious or fearsome.

Seven Stars In the Middle Ages this was a religious sign, being the seven stars in the crown of the Virgin Mary. In later centuries it was thought to be a Masonic symbol with a secret meaning. In some instances, it seems to be derived from the seven stars of Ursa Major. On modern signs, the seven stars sometimes are arranged in a figure seven, sometimes like the heavenly plough or a circle of six with one in the centre.

Shades, Taps and **Vaults** These three words which have separately become the names of pubs, originally meant a kind of small pub for servants. In some cases in the seventeenth century, pubs would have a small pub attached for this purpose. In some cases, these names have survived as rooms in a pub, mostly substituting for the Public Bar.

Shears In the seventeenth century a sheerman was one who was engaged in the trade of cloth-making. Gradually the Shears found its way onto pub signs on inns near the cloth makers, on pubs opened by former sheermen and in sheep shearing areas. The pictorials were sometimes just the shears but sometimes showed a sheep being sheared.

Ship Why do you sometimes see the Ship as a pub sign in the middle of the country on pubs having no obvious relationship with the sea? It could be a pub started by a former seafaring man but it is equally probable that it comes from the time when the Ship referred to Noah's Ark. This was a very popular sign in the later Middle Ages, for religious reasons. Many pubs which were originally called the Ship have changed over the years to be named after a specific ship like the Victory or the Royal George. Yet again this is an example of the evolution of pub names. In time, all memory of the original name, the Ship, let alone Noah's Ark is lost.

Shoulder of Mutton For once, this pub sign, which is surprisingly frequent in the North, means pretty much what it says rather than having heraldic or historic or religious overtones. It mainly comes from a publican having a second way to earn money, butchering. There was one pub in seventeenth-century London by this name with a sign showing St John the Baptist's head in a dish but that unexplained connection seems to be an exception.

Silent Woman This is another name which once honoured beheaded saints but now makes light of the fairer sex, like the Good Woman and the Quiet Woman (see above).

Slug and Lettuce See Red Lattice

Star Yet another sign which, in earlier centuries, was exclusively religious. It represented the Star of Bethlehem and the Nativity or the Star of the Sea, the emblem of the Virgin Mary. And, of course, in the days of illiteracy and crude artists, it was also a very easy sign to paint and to recognize. In later centuries, the Star had heraldic significance, as in Leg and Star, Star and Garter and also sometimes simply meant a star in the sky such as the North Star and the Pole Star.

Strangers' Bar See Hole In The Wall

Sun For once, an ancient sign with Pagan rather than Christian origins. The Sun and the Moon were representatives of Apollo and Diana, popular also because they were easy to portray and recognize. The Sun continued its popularity as a pub sign because it became the badge of Edward III. Of course, the sun is also the source of light for the world as well as heat and life itself so no wonder that it is popular as a pub sign.

Swan The Swan is a very common sign, possibly because it is regal and attractive. In ancient times it was also a symbol of innocence. Normally shown as a white swan (and sometimes called this in the pub name), it also appears as the Black Swan (which locals tend to call the Mucky Duck) and the Swan Revived, perhaps a reference to a pub reopening after its suppression at the Reformation.

Swan with Two Necks It makes for a wonderful picture but it really doesn't mean a swan with two necks but, rather, a swan with two nicks cut into its bill to indicate that it was owned by the Dyer's or Vintner's companies. Ancient documents show that there were over 200 different marks used on the swans' beaks in Lincolnshire to show ownership. Royal swans had five nicks.

Swords Not, in this instance, the name of a pub but rather to mention that sometimes people were named after pubs! It is well known that sections of London are named after pubs (Swiss Cottage, Elephant and Castle, Angel) and streets are even more often named after pubs. But in early days when surnames were not as well defined if they existed at all in a locality, people would be identified by where they lived. Such as, Joyce at the Swords, Paul at the Bell, Jean at the Sun, or John at the Tankard. In time, the 'at the' was dropped and a family name was begun.

Tabard This is one of the most famous inns in history, being the Southwark pub where Chaucer and the other pilgrims began their journey to Canterbury. On the road in front of the pub, there used to be a beam laid crosswise upon two uprights which had this inscription: 'This is the Inne where Sir Jeffrey Chaucer and the nine-and-twenty pilgrims lay in their

The Talbot The Talbot was a breed of hunting hound which looked something like today's Dalmations. It was the crest of the Talbot family, the Earls of Shrewsbury and, for this reason, has provided a name for many pubs. It had remarkable powers of scent which made it such a popular hunting dog. The Talbot painted on this sign is on a relief carving against a bright red background. The three symbols

do not have a direct meaning for this pub but reflect the popularity of three objects on pub signs, whether it be Tuns, Greyhounds, Sailors or whatever. The number three has been important in almost all cultures and religions.

The Talbot Inn is a Freehouse in Much Wenlock, Shropshire, which has been offering accommodation and a warm welcome to travellers and locals for six centuries.

A George Mackenney oil sketch for **The Swan** Overleaf. Mackenney's talent is obvious in this treatment for a **Quart Pot**.

journey to Canterbury, anno 1383'. The name of the pub comes from a garment which was shown on the sign. It was a sleeveless coat, open on both sides, with a square collar. It was a stately garment once worn by noblemen. The pub was reputed in later years to have changed its name and sign to the Talbot but there is no clear evidence of this that I have found.

Talbot The talbot was a popular breed of hunting dog, a kind of hound, white with black spots all over the body and legs. The dog appears on many pub signs even today because it was a favourite of many countrymen and because it was the crest of the Talbot family, the Earls of Shrewsbury. Many of today's signs are believed to have come from that heraldic source rather than directly from this now extinct breed. The talbot was similar to the modern dalmatian hound in appearance.

THE QUART POT

Tankard Why not name the pub after the chief vessel used therein? The Tankard was known as a pub sign as early as the 1400s. The word is from the old French 'tanquard', a large vessel for liquids usually having a cover. The practice of putting lids on tankards is said to be from the beer gardens of Munich and was to keep falling chestnuts out of the beer. The Tankard, the Quart Pot, the Bottle and Glass and other signs depicting the drinking 'tools' of the pubs are still often found today.

Thirteen Cantons The origin of this sign and also the George and Thirteen Cantons and the Sun and Thirteen Cantons dates from the time when many people from Switzerland came to this country to work as servants and settled in Soho in London. These pub signs represent the Thirteen Cantons of Switzerland and reflected the origins of the regulars.

Thistle and Crown The thistle is the emblem of Scotland and the Thistle and Crown or Crown and Thistle was adopted mostly by pubs in the North with some Scottish connection or admiration. The thistle is said to have been adopted to commemorate the unsuccessful attack by the Danes on Stirling Castle in the eighth century and the Order of the Thistle is a Scottish order of Knighthood, ranking second to the Garter in the hierarchy of British orders of chivalry.

Three Alls See Alls

Three Angels The Three Angels may have been intended to represent the angels who appeared to Abraham but three is a very popular number on pub signs and, indeed, throughout history. Almost all religions and cultures revere three. Christianity, of course, has the Trinity. The ancient Chinese said One produced two, Two produced three and Three produced all things. Pythagoras said that three was the perfect number because it indicated the beginning, the middle and the end. Three is also an ideal number for the artistic arrangement of items on heraldic shields, as a study of London Guild arms will show. An interesting variation on the Three signs is the Three Loggerheads on which two are painted, the third being the onlooker reading the sign. Therefore a pub being named and signed the Three Somethings may not have a specific meaning for the number three, just this general meaning.

Three Jolly Butchers This sign might have an explanation as above but it also might have a reference to three north-country butchers who killed nine highwaymen according to ballad and legend.

Three Kings This is generally considered to be a religious sign having nothing to do with British kings. The Three Kings honours the Magi who came to greet the infant Jesus bearing gifts of gold, frankincense and myrrh.

Three Tuns The Three Tuns is a popular sign because the three tuns appear on the coat of arms of the Vintners Company. A tun is a wooden barrel larger than a man. Again three because it is artistically balanced on a shield.

Tucker's Grave Hopefully, this story won't put you off your beer! It has two versions. Tucker's Grave is a pub between Radstock and Trowbridge, Wilts, and would remind the visitor of pubs of an earlier time. There is no bar. The beer and cider are drawn from the barrel and locals sit around what looks like an ale-wife's kitchen. Tucker was a rough gent in the 1700s. When he got in trouble, he went away and was gone for many years, then to return unknown and broke. He hanged himself in a barn and is buried under the pub's car park. The other version has the same Tucker killing and burying customers under what is now the car park. From the peaceful pub of today, you would never guess its history.

Tumbledown Dick This sign is said to have originated as a satirical comment on the fall from power of Richard Cromwell, the son of the Protector. Tumbledown meant anything that was upset, falling and breaking or falling down drunk. Hence one such pub sign which showed Diogenes on one side and a drunken man on the other with the inscription, 'Now Diogenes is dead and laid in his tomb, Tumble-down Dick is come in his room'.

Turk's Head In addition to being another name for the Saracen's Head (see above), it also comes from a similar source. From the·fifteenth to the seventeenth century, the Turks were feared throughout Europe and prayers were said to prevent the Turks from invading. So, again, they were shown as evil, frightening men.

Twin Foxes See Fox

Two Brewers This is also sometimes known as the Jolly Brewers and often shows two men carrying a barrel of beer suspended from a pole. With that image, it is a direct descendant of the Roman sign for a vintner: two men carrying an amphora suspended from a pole. The number two appears on pub signs frequently but does not appear to have any special meaning.

Two Cocks See Fighting Cocks

Uncle Tom There is still at least one Uncle Tom's Cabin in Britain, this one being in Blackpool. It was once on a number of pubs throughout the country. It seems that Harriet Beecher Stowe's novel inspired all sorts of small, inaccessible pubs to adopt the name. In addition to this and Robin Hood, many pubs have commemorated literature, fable and ballad. There were Robinson Crusoes, Jim Crows, Toby Philpotts and Old Rosons to be found in earlier times.

Under the Rose In addition to the Rose pub signs mentioned earlier, there were pubs named Under the Rose. In this case it was not the colour or kind of rose that was important but that a rose be painted on the ceiling. There was an old belief that whatever conversations were held under the rose would be kept confidential and never divulged.

Unicorn The unicorn probably came to pub signs after being on other signs, as it was often used by chemists and goldsmiths. There are numerous mentions of this fabled animal in the Old Testament and it was mentioned by Ctesias in 400 BC. It was said that the only way to catch a unicorn was to have a lovely young virgin rest in one of his known haunts. The unicorn would rush to her, put his head in her lap and sleep and, thus, be captured. Because the unicorn would rest in the lap of a virgin, early Christians chose him to represent Christ, born of the Virgin Mary. It was believed that dipping the horn of a unicorn in liquid would determine whether it contained any poison and powdered horn was considered to be an aphrodisiac. These beliefs led to the Unicorn being a sign for chemists and apothecaries. The unicorn appears on the arms of the Goldsmiths, Wax Chandlers and Apothecaries Companies and also occurs on the royal badge of Scotland. The arms of James I had two unicorns.

Union Pubs with this name are honouring one or more of several unions. The first was the union of England and Wales in 1536. About 140 years later, the first Union sign was noted, on a London coffee house. The next union was with Scotland in 1707 and finally came the union with Ireland in 1801. The choice of Union for a pub name can also be traced to two pubs with different names being merged.

Vaults The word vaults was originally a synonym for cellars because a medieval cellar was normally vaulted. It came to mean a cool storage room for beers and wines and was an alternative name for 'tap'. In Victorian times, some pubs were known by the owner's name, as in Peters' Vaults for a pub owned by a Thomas and Marianne Peters. The use of Vaults meaning pub was much more common in the North of England where the name still is in use. In other instances, the name has gone from describing a part (the cellar) to the whole (the pub) and back to a part since it is often used in place of Public Bar. Vault could also mean a pub or room in a pub for servants, see Shades, Taps and Vaults.

Vine The Vine is an obvious sign for a pub, particularly one which specializes in wines. This name is synonymous with and sometimes exchanged with the Bunch of Grapes. Pubs called the Vine might also owe their name to being in an area where grape vines were once planted, especially in London and the South East.

Vintners Arms The Vintners Company was formally incorporated in 1436 or 1437 although it had existed in some form for several hundred years. It was granted arms in 1447, 'Sable a chevron between three wine tuns argent'. The Vintners Company was one of the twelve great Livery Companies of the City of London. This is a natural sign for a pub although it is probably more frequently seen as simply the Three Tuns.

Virgin See Our Lady

Vulcan Since Vulcan is the god of fire, he was the patron of the smiths. Since smithing is such thirsty work, this became a popular sign, particularly in the Black Country. Other gods are also honoured on signs, including Neptune, Cupid and Mercury.

WHITE HORSE

A simple but effective Mackenney oil sketch shows his skill with horses.

Vulture Understandably a less frequent sign, given the reputation of vultures! Before the Great Fire, there was a live sign of the Vulture in Cornhill, featuring a vulture in a cage. The house was consumed in the flames but there is no word on the fate of the vulture. The pub was rebuilt as the George and Vulture.

Waggon and Horses This is a sign still frequently seen in the countryside. It dates from the seventeenth century when the country carriers would travel to and from London with their horse-drawn waggons, stopping in towns along the way to collect and deliver goods.

Waving Flag Probably every kind of soldier, sailor and airman, all of their uniforms and regiments are represented on pub signs. If not at pubs near barracks or other military haunts then at pubs run by the ex-military man. But even more popular are the Standard, the Banner or the Waving Flag. In one way or another, the vast majority of pub names and signs are patriotic. In addition to these are all of the signs related to royalty, kings' and queens' heads and arms, flowers and shields and heraldic devices.

Well and Bucket A very old sign, mentioned as early as 1472, the Well and Bucket comforts the pub patron with the image of an inexhaustible supply of beverage.

Wheatsheaf The wheatsheaf figures on the arms of the Bakers Company and is a popular sign with pubs. It was once also a regularly seen sign for bakers. It has been said that some pubs with this sign also baked on the same premises and combined these two staffs of life in one business.

White Boar See Blue Boar

White Hart The white hart was the favourite badge of Richard II and most so-named pub signs are influenced by that. But the white hart is not always shown as the heraldic animal. He is sometimes painted realistically. Frequently, the white hart has a golden collar or a gold chain around his neck. This stems from the legend, as reported by Aristotle, that Diomedes consecrated a white hart to Diana and placed a collar of gold around its neck. The same basic story has been told with different casts – Julius Caesar, Alexander the Great, Charlemagne and Henry the Lion.

White Horse There are many reasons why this is such a popular sign throughout Britain. First must be the British love of horses since many of these signs are either a locally well known horse or just a generalized white horse. But the White Horse was the standard of the Saxons, the badge of Kent (related to the white horses cut in the chalk of hills) and a device of the House of Hanover. It also appears on the emblazonments of the Carmen, Coachmakers, Farriers, Innholders, Saddlers and Wheelwrights.

White House There is still at least one White House, painted pink, in London today. This has nothing to do with the American president's official residence although the sign may depict that famous White House. Rather it is another example of a description of the pub becoming the name and then the sign either echoing the building or, as mentioned, showing another White House. As a pub name it easily pre-dates Teddy Roosevelt's naming of the American one.

White Swan While most swans on pub signs are painted white, the pubs are more often just called the Swan. But there are some specific White Swans, probably first so-named to honour Edward III who placed the device of a White Swan on his shield for a tournament at Canterbury in 1349.

Whittington and His Cat Pubs probably should think twice before honouring Dick Whittington. As Lord Mayor of London during the third time he held that post, 1419–20, he led a crusade against ale-sellers, fining them heavily. But Sir Richard Whittington and his undoubtedly fictional cat live on in story and pantomime . . . and on pub signs.

Who'd A Thought It This comes from several sources but its always an expression of surprise. For example, when the local baker, after years of trying and being rejected, gets a licence to open a pub, his friends said, Who'd a Thought It! Or when a publican was revealed to have become wealthy from running his pub, a similar cry went up.

Woolpack While the Woolpack and the Woolsack may seem to be different versions of the same sign, they are quite different. The Woolpack is a pack of wool weighing 240 lbs while a Woolsack is simply a sack of wool of any weight. These signs grew popular in wool producing areas and also reflect the importance of wool in the country's economy for centuries.

World's End Not to worry, this sign is not a prediction. In fact, its meaning has been lost for the most part. Pubs called the World's End were usually at the edge of a village or town and inhabitants rarely went beyond them, hence the name.

World Turned Upside Down Meaning that things are the opposite of what is right and natural, this is a very old pub name and sign. There are many stories as to its origin. Among them are that it was said by prisoners being sent to Australia, that it stemmed from the discovery of the South Pole and that it was the music played by the British band when the Americans won their Revolutionary War. Artists usually have fun with this sign, showing rabbits chasing dogs or horses riding in carriages or mice scaring cats.

X Named Pubs As far as I could discover, there are currently no pub names starting with 'X'. There was an XL in Garstang, Lancashire. It referred both to one of the brewers' strong beers and to 'excell'. But the pub now has a new name. There was an 'XX' in Manchester and, for a time, an 'X' in Westcott.

Yew Tree The frequency of this sign is because the wood of the yew tree was used to make the bows that did such damage at Agincourt and Poitiers and wherever else the English fought before gunpowder. The yew tree also figured in at least one awful punning sign. This Yew Tree had a publican named Newberry and his sign showed some berries on the tree and a golden 'N' resting on a branch: N-yew-berry.

Zetland This London pub was named after a famous warship of the past and, perhaps, to capitalize on the fact that 'Z' pubs are rare and therefore more memorable. Others are the Zebra in Cambridge, Zodiak in Ashford, Kent and Zanty Arms in Liverpool.

Chapter 7

THE BEST IN BRITAIN

The pub signs listed here are excellent ones discovered by the author when researching this book. They are the author's favourites and ones recommended by friends, publicans, brewers, artists and any other source he could find. So, before you become upset at what is not included, please turn to the Final Note after this chapter.

It is the author's strong belief that a good pub sign leads to a good pub. The reverse is not always true, as some good pubs have poor signs. But, more often than not, good signs and good pubs go together. Why? Because the good sign is an immediate notice that somebody cares about the pub and is making the effort to make an excellent pub in every way possible. That somebody can be the brewers or the publican – or both because, again, they go together.

The following listings, organized by county and city or town, will give you a starting point. Visit the pubs listed, see what *you* think of the pub sign, what *you* think of the pub. Cheers!

AVON
Bath Britannia
Box Queen's Head
Bristol Silks ·
Bristol Printer's Devil
Bristol Old Duke
Bristol Beaufort
Bristol Jolly Cobbler
Bristol Elephant
Bristol Princes Bar
Bristol Windbound
Bristol Sedan Chair
Bristol Glasscutter
Calne Talbot
Chippenham Royal Oak
Chipping Sudbury
   Grapes
Marlborough Five Alls

BEDFORDSHIRE
Bedford Perseverance
Kempston Hardwick
   Chimney Corner
Luton Lute and Tun
Luton Wabbit
Luton Boater
Old Warden Hare and
   Hounds
Sharnbrook Swan with
   Two Nicks

BERKSHIRE
Blacknest Chukka
Windsor Court Jester
Windsor Old Trout

BUCKINGHAM-
SHIRE
Aston Clinton Rising
   Sun
Bishopstone Harrow
Chesham Red Lion
Denham Falcon
Denham Green Man
Hurley Black Boy
Turville Bull and
   Butcher

CAMBRIDGESHIRE
Cambridge Zebra
Winchelsea Straw Bear

CHESHIRE
Barbridge Barbridge
   Inn
Bebington Rose and
   Crown
Bebington Wellington
Bromborough Royal
   Oak
Chester Snooty Fox
Chester Telford's
   Warehouse
Hoo Green Kilton
Knutsford Smoker
Macclesfield·Cat and
   Fiddle
Macclesfield Legh
   Arms/Black Boy
Mobberley Frozen
   Mop

The Rifle Volunteer

Surprisingly, there are a number of pubs so named throughout Britain. They honour a time when warfare was still almost an amateur pastime. A Rifle Volunteer had to obtain his own rifle and then find someone to teach him how to shoot it before he could join the army. This pictorial of a determined young volunteer was painted by Norman Hartley Signs of Manchester.

The Rifle Volunteer is a Wilson's pub at Bredbury, near Stockport, Cheshire.

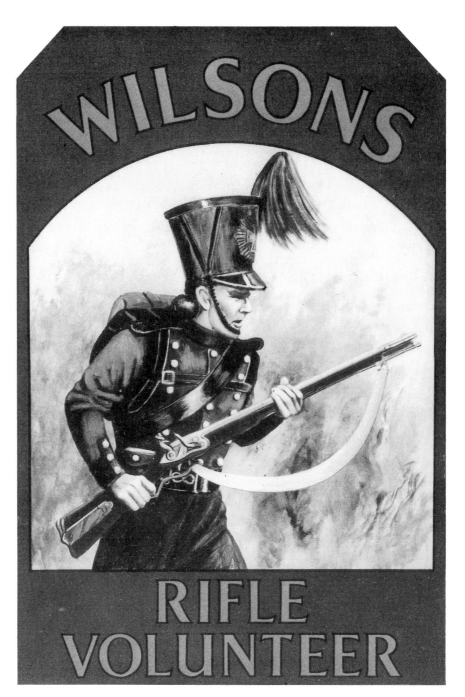

Sandbach Sandpiper
Southport Volunteer
Stockport The
    Crossings
Stockport Ring O'
    Bells

CORNWALL
Delabole Bettle and
    Chisel
Newquay King Mork
Porth Cornish Clough
Porthtowan Porpoise
Saltash Brunel
St Issey Ring O' Bells
Truro Britannia
Truro Coach and
    Horses

CUMBRIA
Aspatria Letters Inn
Bowness-on-
    Windermere John
    Peel
Carlisle Post
Carlisle Woolpack
Gosforth Red Admiral
Sawrey Tower Bank
    Arms
Threlkeld Salutation
    Hotel
The Green, Lynne

DERBYSHIRE
Creswell Black
    Diamond
Hurdlow Bull i' th'
    Thorn

DEVON
Bickington Toby Jug
Cockington Drum
Cowley Three
    Horseshoes
Crockernwell Judge
    Jeffries
Holcombe Smugglers
    Inn
Kentisbeare Keeper's
    Cottage

Plympton Unicorn
Princetown Plume of
    Feathers
Thorverton Dolphin
Tiverton Prince
    Blucher
Wrangaton Wounded
    Soldier

DORSET
Coldharbour Silent
    Woman
Gillingham Buffalo
Marnhull Blackmore
    Vale
Piddletrenthide Piddle
    Inn
Poole St Peters Finger
Portstone Dorset
    Knob
Stalbridge Q
Tolpuddle Martyrs
Wareham Cock and
    Bottle
Weymouth Admiral
    Hardy
Wimborne Winston
    Churchill

DURHAM
Hartlepool
    Fisherman's Arms

ESSEX
Canvey Island Admiral
    Jellicoe
Chelmsford
    Endeavour
Colchester Cups
Colchester Odd One
    Out
Colchester Prettygate
Colchester Wig and
    Figet
Harlow Dusty Miller
Harlow Purple
    Emperor
Hastingswood
    Common The
    Rainbow and Dove

Manningtree Wooden
    Fender
Saffron Walden Eight
    Bells
South Benfleet Half
    Crown
Stansted Abbot
    Queen's Head
Stanway Live and Let
    Live
Theydon Bois Sixteen
    String Jack
Upminster Golden
    Crane

GLOUCESTER-
SHIRE
Amberley Black Horse
Aylburton George
Aylburton Common
    Besom
Bourton on the Water
    Coach and Horses
Brierley Swan
Cheltenham Jolly
    Brewmaster
Cheltenham
    Leckhampton
Gloucester Great
    Western
Little Barrington Inn
    for All Seasons
Nailsworth Tipputs
Quenington Keeper's
    Arms
Stroud Butcher's
    Arms
Teddington
    Teddington Hands
Tewkesbury Gupshill
    Manor

GREATER
MANCHESTER
Manchester Victoria
Manchester Jolly
    Angler
Solihull Spitfire
Staley Bridge British
    Protection

Wigan White Crow
Worsley Pied Piper

HAMPSHIRE
Clanfield Bat and Ball
Denmead Forest of
  Bere
Micheldever Lunways
New Milton Speckled
  Trout
Portsmouth Electric
  Arms
Portsmouth Fifth
  Hampshire
  Volunteers Arms
Southampton
  Talisman
Southampton Honest
  Lawyer

HEREFORD &
  WORCESTER
Cleobury Mortimer
  Old Lion
Earl's Croome Gay
  Dog
Evesham Golden
  Heart
Hereford Cock of
  Tupsley
Ross on Wye Eagle
Roxhill Shepherd's
  Rest

HERTFORDSHIRE
Barley Fox and
  Hounds
Berkhamsted
  Brownlow Arms
Berkhamsted Kings
  Arms
Birchanger Three
  Willows
Codicote Globe
Dobbs Weir Fish and
  Eels
Frithsden Alford Arms
Great Hallingbury
  Hop Pole
Hatfield Comet

The Teddington Hands The
Teddington Hands pub stands
right at the crossroads in
Teddington. Just next to the pub
is an old stone post with 'hands'
pointing to the nearby towns. In
this case, the pub has not only
been named after a local
landmark but has actually
become part of that landmark.
Anyone mentioning the
Teddington hands would be
referred to all three.
  The Teddington Hands is a
Flowers pub near Tewkesbury,
Gloucestershire.

Hemel Hempstead
  Crown and Sceptre
Hemel Hempstead
  New Venture
Hoddesdon
  Kingfisher
Kempston Slaters
  Arms
Little Gaddesden
  Bridgewater Arms
Potters Crouch Holly
  Bush
Sawbridgeworth
  Queen's Head
St Albans Jolly Sailor
St Albans Fighting
  Cocks
Water End Red Lion
Wicken Bonhunt
  Coach and Horses

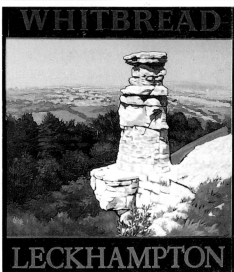

HUMBERSIDE
Thwing Rampant
Horse

ISLE OF WIGHT
Chale Clarendon and
Wight Mouse
Newport Castle Inn
West Cowes Harbour
Lights

KENT
Edenbridge Crown
Gabriels Hill Bull
Island Road Shrew
Beshrewed
Marshside Gate
Old Romney Rose and
Crown
Penbury Black Horse
Plucks Gutter Dog
and Duck
Rusthall Brahms and
Lizst
Stalisfield Green
Plough
Ulcombe Harrow
Warden Point
Wheatsheaf
West Malling Startled
Saint
Worth Blue Pigeon

LANCASHIRE
Ashton-under-Lyne
March Hare
Bamber Bridge
Hospital Inn
Blackburn
Myerscough
Blackburn Dog
Blackburn Stop & Rest
Carnforth
Highwayman
Chorley Top Lock
Cockerham Bridge Inn
Euxton Talbot
Galgate Slip Inn
Heapery Red Cat
Incol Falkland Heroes

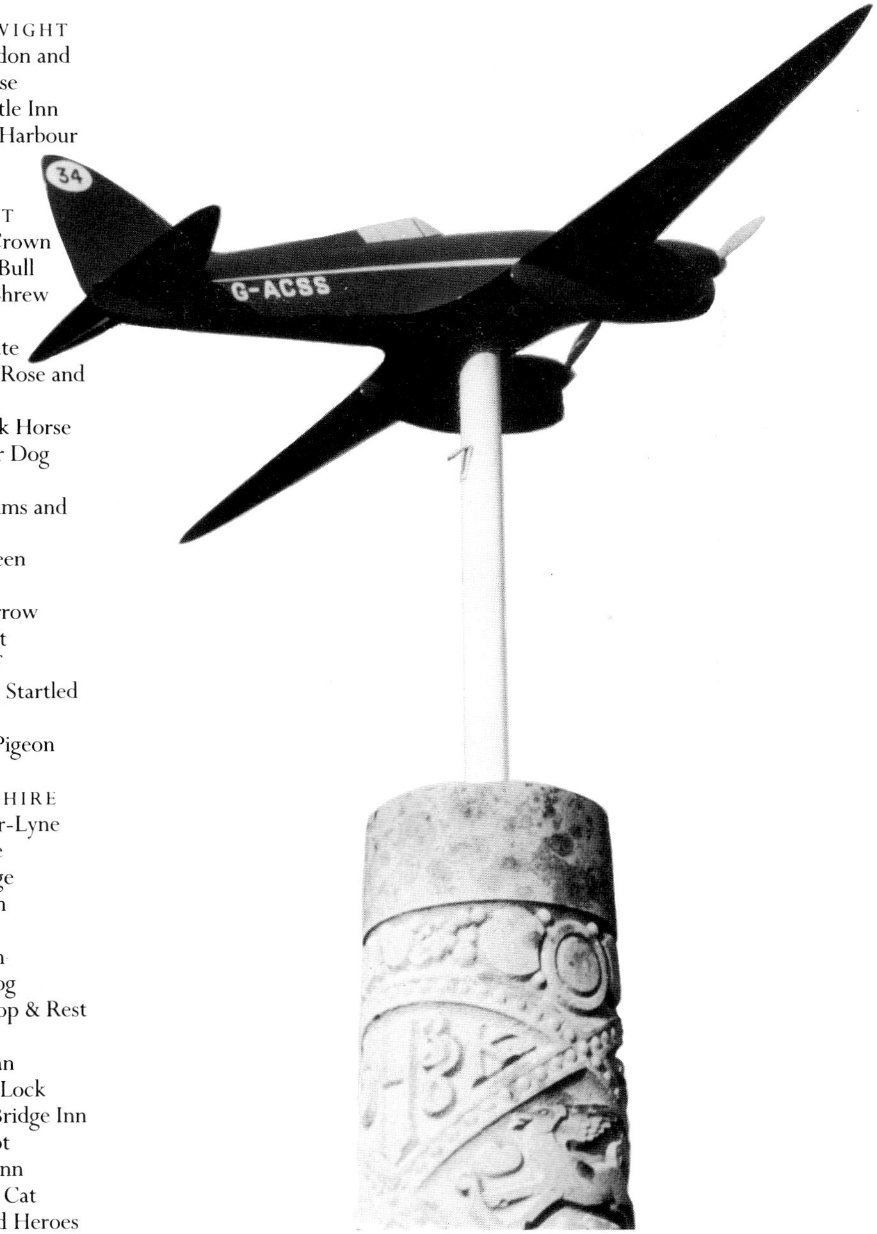

Below left. A geographical treatment for **The Leckhampton**, Cheltenham. Right. **The Comet**, Hatfield.

The Boot The obvious reason for a pub to be called the Boot is that its founder had something to do with boots, perhaps was a bootmaker. In past centuries, pubs were sometimes combined with other retail establishments (as is still done in Ireland) and a bootmaker/pub would become known as the Boot because, typically, a bootmaker would hang a boot as his sign. This Boot was painted by Gaye Lockwood. It has won a major design award and the sign was exhibited in Paris and London before it was hung.

The Boot is a Tolly Cobbold pub in Freston in Suffolk.

Kendal Yorkshire House
Lancaster Victorian
Lancaster Merchant
Lancaster Ring O' Bells
Lancaster New Inn
Lancaster Three Mariners
Lancaster Rose
Lancaster Greaves Hotel
Lancaster Tramway
Morecombe Manor Inn
Morecombe Joiners Arms
Orrell Kingfisher
Parbold Farmers Arms
Preston Running Pump
Preston Dr Syntax
Tatham Fleece

LINCOLNSHIRE
Stamford George

NORFOLK
Acle Bridge
Briston Green Man
Dersingham Feathers
Great Yarmouth Gallon Pot
Kings Lynn London Porterhouse
Norwich Hog in Armour
Thetford Anchor
Winterton-on-Sea Fisherman's Return

NORTHAMPTON-SHIRE
Northampton Double Four
Northampton

Hopping Hill
Stony Stratford Cock
Stony Stratford Bull

NOTTINGHAM-SHIRE
Nottingham Gardens

OXFORDSHIRE
Botley Fair Rosamund
Dorchester George
Highmoor Dog and Duck
Milton Common Three Pigeons
Oxford Eagle and Child
Oxford Trout
South Stoke Perch and Pike
Stoke Row Crooked Billet

The Wherryman This is one of two sigs hanging in the Victoria and Albert Museum's gift shop! This is an opportunity to see the work a great English artist did on a pub sign. John Crome, often known as Old Crome to distinguish him from his painter son, lived from 1768 to 1821. He was apprenticed to a Norwich sign painter, Francis Whisler, at the age of fourteen and is known to have painted a number of signs. He then went to London but later returned to his native city and became the leading figure in the 'Norwich School' of painting. Pub sign histories say that a painting of Old Crome's, the Jolly Sailor, was for a pub sign. The sign was moved inside the pub at Yarmouth and, in 1906, it was sold at an auction for twelve guineas. What is called the Jolly Sailor is probably this Wherryman. Even in the V & A, it is informally called the Jolly Sailor.

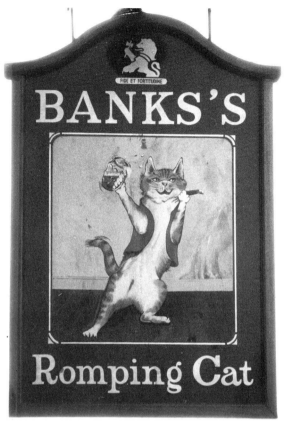

The Romping Cat Pub names and pub sign pictorials can go through a series of evolutionary changes which leave the original name long forgotten. This pub was once one of the thousand or so pubs in Britain with a Red Lion sign, even though its name was the Sandbank Tavern. Some years ago and for a reason now unknown, the name was changed to the Rampant Cat. In virtually any pub you can find some regulars who delight in twisting the pub name (The Boar's Head becomes the Whore's Bed, the Crown and Sceptre becomes the Cap and Snake) and sometimes the altered name sticks. Hence, the Romping Cat.

The Romping Cat is a Wolverhampton and Dudley Breweries' Bank's pub in Bloxwich, Birmingham. The cigar-smoking, beer-drinking cat was painted by John Matthews.

SALOP (SHROPSHIRE)
Bewdley Duke William
Much Wenlock George & Dragon
Much Wenlock Talbot
Much Wenlock Royal Oak
Oswestry Last Inn
Oswestry Ye Olde Boote Inn
Shrewsbury Dog & Bull
Stourport-on-Severn Wheatsheaf

SOMERSET
Cannington Friendly Spirit
Chard George
Chilton Polden Toby
Crewkerne Kings Arms
Hambridge Lion and Lamb
Misterton White Swan
Southover Full Moon
Taunton Four Alls

STAFFORDSHIRE
Brookhouse Huntsman
Cheadle Huntsman
Leek Quiet Woman
Newcastle Albert Inn
Rugeley Chadwick Arms
Stoke-on-Trent Potter
Stoke-on-Trent Forest Tavern
Stoke-on-Trent Bulls Head
Stoke-on-Trent Noah's Ark
Stoke-on-Trent Robin Hood

SUFFOLK
Clare Swan

SURREY
Addlestone Magnet
Bletchingley White Hart
Earlswood Common Albatross
Farncombe Three Lions
Farnham Pride of the Valley
Godalming Kings Arms and Royal
Guildford Cannon
Guildford Rats Castle
Guildford King's Head
Guildford Two Brewers
Guildford Greyhound
Horsell Bleak House
Horsell Plough
Leigh Seven Stars
Nonarchy Duke of Nonarch
Pinbright White Hart
Smithbrock Leathern Bottle
Stane Street Old School House
Staines Jolly Butcher
Woking Red House
Woking Sovereign

EAST SUSSEX
Argos Hill Bicycle
Brighton Sir Charles Napier
Hever Henry VIII
Marefield Chequers
Milton Street Sussex Ox
Northiam Crown and Thistle
Willington British Queen

WEST SUSSEX
Bedhampton Golden Lion
Chichester Globe
Effingham Lord Howard

The Drovers' Arms, Newport, Gwent.

Horsham Bear
Horsham Dog and
  Bacon
Horsham Green
  Dragon
Horsham Queen's
  Head
Horsham Rising Sun
Mickleham Running
  Horses

Nutborne
  Barleycorn
Pease Pottage James
  King
Shipley George and
  Dragon
Tangmere Bader Arms
Tillington
  Horseguards
Tirsley Green

Greyhound
Worth Parsons Pig

TYNE AND WEAR
Blaydon Sporting
  Arms

WARWICKSHIRE
Stratford-upon-Avon
  Sportsman

WEST MIDLANDS
Birmingham Tipsy
  Gent
Bloxwich Romping Cat
Brierley Hill Lame
  Dog
Dudley King and
  Queen
Kings Norton
  Navigation

Stourbridge Labour in
  Vain
Walsall Pretty Bricks

WILTSHIRE
Calne Talbot
Luckington Old Royal
  Ship
Marlborough Five Alls
Marlborough Golden Ball

154

The Haverstock Arms While it does not relate to the name of the pub, this full-wall painting is the pub sign for the Haverstock Arms. A local artist was commissioned to paint this mural which brightens up an otherwise dull flank wall. The main advantage of the sign is that it is clearly visible to motorists driving down a long hill toward the pub, giving them plenty of time to respond to the peaceful invitation.

The Haverstock Arms is a Charrington pub on Haverstock Hill in London.

NORTH YORKSHIRE
Masham Blackburn in Paradise
Pickering Lettered' Board
Selby Queen's Vaults
Sowerby Bridge Long Chimney

SOUTH YORKSHIRE
Pontefract Chequers
Whitby First In, Last Out

WALES
Anglesey Four Crosses
Anglesey Gazell Hotel
Caerphilly Railway
Cumbran Kingfisher
Llandrindad Wells Happy Union
Newport Drover's Arms

SCOTLAND
Ballindalloch Croft Inn
Cupar Drokit Dug
Edinburgh Cramond Inn
Edinburgh Toll Gate
Edinburgh Valentines
Edinburgh Deacon Brodies

GUERNSEY
English and Guernsey
Hangman's Inn
Jamaica Inn
Thomas de la Rue
Wayside Cheer Hotel

JERSEY
Castle Green
Customs
Harvest Barn
Mermaid
Post Horn

LONDON
Acton W3 Capel Arms
Aldergate Bull and Mouth
Battersea High Street Original Woodman
Belsize George Washington
Blackfriars Blackfriars
Blackhorse Road N5 Woodbine
Camden Hawley Arms
Carnaby Street Shakespeare's Head
Chelsea Goat in Boots
Chiswick Fox and Hounds and Mawson Arms
Clerkenwell Pickled Egg
Dames Road E7 Forest Glen
Fapis Court Road W8 Hanson Cab
Finchley O'Henerys
Green Lanes White Horse
Haverstock Hill NW3 Haverstock Arms
Hemingford Road Huntingdon Arms
High Street E15 Two Brewers
Holborn Oarsman
Lambs Conduit Lamb
Long Acre Sugarloaf
Long Lane SE1 George
Marylebone Globe
Mayfair Running Footman
North End Way NW3 Hare & Hounds
off Fleet Street Cartoonist
Putney Builders Arms
Snowfields SE1 Rose
St Johns Wood NW8 3rd Mrs Gioconda
Upper Norwood The Rising Sun

A book like this is very frustrating for me because it is limited to what I have seen, read about and been told about. While I have had a pint in some 2200 pubs, all in the cause of research you understand, that means I still lack the knowledge of about 80,000 more!

And that is where *you* come in. If you disagree with anything in this book, or agree with something or want to share your favourite pub sign or artist or pub, please do write to me. I will be more than happy to include your information in future editions of this book. And if you want to disagree with something, especially the stories behind the signs, that will give me a corrected or additional story to tell.

Finally I'd love to hear from readers because I enjoy learning about and talking about pubs, pub signs and their histories.

B i b l i o g r a p h y

Many of these books are more about pubs than pub signs *per se* while others are mainly about beer. But almost all of them shed some light on the subject of pub signs. Beyond that, all are very readable and helpful to anyone interested in beer, pubs and pub signs.

For the serious student of pub signs, the place to start is *The History of Signboards* by Larwood and Hotten. First published in 1866, an updated version was published in 1985. While it only contains black and white photographs and relatively few of those, it has a wealth of information on sign history and the signs most popular in the last century and before.

Berry, George, *Taverns and Tokens of Pepys' London* (Seaby Publications 1978)
Besley, Rupert, *Going for a Pint* (Pop Universal, 1985)
Bottomley, Frank, *The Inn Explorer's Guide* (Kaye & Ward, 1984)
Brabbs, Derry, *English Country Pubs*, (Weidenfeld & Nicolson 1986)
Bruning, Ted and Paulin, Keith, *Historic English Inns* (David and Charles, 1982)
Burke, John, *The English Inn*, (B. T. Batsford, 1981)
Burton, Anthony, *Opening Time*, (Unwin Hyman, 1987)
Clark, Peter, *The English Alehouse*, (Longman, 1983)
Davis, Ben, *The Traditional English Pub*, (The Architectural Press, 1981)
Delderfield, Eric R. *British Inn Signs*, (E.R.D. Publications, 1965)
Duddington, C.L., *Plain Man's Guide to Beer* (Pelham Books, 1974)
Dunkling, Leslie, *The Guinness Book of Names*, (Guinness Books, 1974)
Dunkling, Lesie and Wright, Gordon, *A Dictionary of Pub Names* (Routledge & Kegan Paul, 1987)
Foster, Terence, *Dr Foster's Book of Beer*, (Adam and Charles Black, 1979)
Girouard, Mark, *Victorian Pubs*, (Yale University Press, 1984)
Glover, Brian, *CAMRA Dictionary of Beer*, (Longman, 1985)
Gorham, Maurice and Dunnett, H.McG., *Inside the Pub*, (The Architectural Press, 1950)
Hackwood, Frederick W., *Inns, Ales and Drinking Customs of Old England*, (Bracken Books, 1909)
Hogg, Garry, *The English Country Inn*, (B.T. Batsford, 1974)
Jackson, Michael, *The World Guide to Beer*, (The Apple Press, 1977)
Keverne, Richard, *Tales of Old Inns*, (Collins, 1939)

Lamb, Cadbury, *Inn Signs*, (Shire Publications, 1976)

Larwood, Jacob and Hotten, John Camden, *The History of Signboards*, (John Camden Hotten, 1866)

Lillywhite, Bryant, *London Signs*, (George Allen and Unwin, 1972)

McGill, Angus, *Pub*, (Longmans, 1969)

Mayle, Peter, *More Time, Gentlemen, Please*, (Andre Deutsch, 1984)

Monckton, H.A., *The Story of The British Pub*, (Publishing & Literary Services, 1982)

Monson-Fitzjohn, G.J., *Quaint Signs of Olde Inns* (Herbert Jenkins, 1926)

Noakes, Aubrey and Fyson, Nance Lui, *London Pride*, (Jupiter, 1978)

Playfair, Guy Lyon, *The Haunted Pub Guide*, (Harrap, 1985)

Popham, H.E. *The Guide to London Taverns*, (Claud Stacey, 1927)

Richardson, A.E., *The Old Inns of England*, (B.T. Batsford, 1934)

Robertson, James D. *The Connoisseur's Guide to Beer*, (Green Hill Publishers, 1983)

Whipple, Andy and Anderson, Rob, *The English Pub*, (Viking, 1985)

A c k n o w l e d g e m e n t s

A book of this kind cannot be done without a lot of help from a lot of people. There is a great fear that I will miss thanking and acknowledging someone. (If I do, forgive me and thanks for your help). First, some general thanks which will, I hope, include anyone otherwise not mentioned.

To all of the authors of the books on pubs, pub signs and signs in general I have read: thanks for the pleasure I've had and the things I have learned.

To all the artists who have so graciously shared their work and to the brewers and publicans for pointing me towards good signs and filling in all the background information. In this regard, two things should be noted. All of the photographs which were made available for the book (and not taken by the author) are acknowledged under the photo. The copyright for all of the original art shown in this book remains with the artists or the breweries.

My final general thanks are to all of the individuals, many of them in the Holly Bush and The Alford Arms, who have given ideas, mentioned good signs they have seen and asked questions which helped the book.

Specifically, my thanks go to: Laura Corballis and Roger deWolf for research help; Megan Dutt for incidental artwork; Robert Weber of the Brewer's Society for his knowledge, help and for correcting my worst mistakes; the Hemel Business Centre in Hemel Hempstead for typing, secretarial and mailing help; Berkhamsted Photographic for developing, printing and guidance; the friends who fed me and loaned me beds, cars and meeting spaces (notably Robin & Val Corbett, Judy Wade, Peter & Christine Matthews, Tim & Bunty Gilligan, Jim & Betty Kerby and The Fins); the friendly and helpful staff of the Lower Red Lion in St Albans where much of the work was prepared; Mary and Peter Hugens for reading and reacting to the first draft; George and Thelma Mackenney for their friendship and for the invaluable art appreciation lessons they unknowingly gave me.

Finally, my thanks to Charlie Frusher, the late publican at The Cock and Bottle for giving me my first pub sign.

Adam and Eve, The   89
Albion, The   89
Ale-garland   14, 29
   see also garland
Ale-house   11, 12, 14
ale-stake   12, 33
Alls, various   89, 91
Alma, The   90
Anchor, The   90, 92
Angel, The   34, 90, 139
animals (in general)   15, 78, 86, 87, 99, 117
Anne, Queen   33, 88
Anstey, The Crown   97
Argyle, Duchess of   48, 49
arms, coats of   90, 92, 107, 116, 119
Artichoke, The   90
Ashbourne, The Green Man and Black's Head   17, 20
Ashridge House   14

Barley Mow, The   47
Bass Charrington brewery   80, 81
Bayeux Tapestry   12, 13, 100
Bear, The   91
Beehive, The   91
beer, origins of   10
Beetle, The   91
Bell, The   91, 101
Berkhamsted, The King's Arms   88
Bettws-y-Coed, The Royal Oak   41
birds (in general)   29, 31, 91
Birmingham, The Romping Cat   152
Birmingham, The Tipsy Gent   86
Bishop, The   91
Boar, The   92
Bottle, The   98, 111
Boulogne Mouth, The   34, 50, 86, 92
Bredbury, The Rifle Volunteer   146
Brewers, The   140
breweries, involvement of   69, 70, 80
Brewery Artists Limited   77, 78, 79
Bricks, The   119
Bristol, Silks   87
Browne, Thomas   17
Bucket, The   143

Bull, The   91, 92
Butcher, The   139

Canton, The   139
Case is Altered, The   85, 86, 88
Castle, The   101
Cat, The   99, 114, 144
Catherine, Saint   99
Chamberlain, Lord   15
Charles II, King   35, 45, 71, 87, 101, 109, 132
Chaucer, Geoffrey   31
   see also Tabard
Chequers, The   11, 35, 47, 97, 98
Chesham brewery   8
Chew, Stanley   80, 81
church, influence of   13, 91, 113
Cirencester, Abbots of   31
Clarence, Duke of   91
Cock, The   98, 101, 106
Cockle, John   48
Colnbrook, The Ostrich   15
Compass, The   90, 105
Cooper, Alfred   52
Cooper, Len   72, 73, 74
Courage brewery   72, 74, 80, 81
Cow, The   100
Cowper, William   7
Cox, David   40
Crane, The   98
Crane, Walter   46
Crome, John Berney   45, 52, 151
Crooked Billet, The   97
Crown, The   97, 139

design companies   74, 75, 77, 79
Devil, The   112
Dog, The   91, 99, 102, 110, 114
   (see also Talbot)
Dragon, The   100
Duck, The   100
Dwarf, The   100

Eagle, The   100
Edgar, King   14

Edward III, King   33, 143
Elephant   101
Elizabeth Georgiana, Lady   48, 49
Elizabeth I, Queen   15, 33, 101, 109, 115
Ellis, Ralph   38
estates, influence of   13, 14
exhibitions of pub sign art   38, 46, 48

Falcon, The   101
Farmer, The   73
Feathers, The   101
Fiddle, The   99
Fish, The   101
Flag, The   143
Fleece, The   102
Fleur de Lys, The   101
Footman, The   133
Foster, Miles Birket   52
Fountain, The   97
Fox, The   81, 102, 103, 107
Freston, The Boot   150

Gainsborough, Thomas   33
gallows signs   17, 31
Garland   102
George, Saint   102, 104, 113, 134
Globe   104, 105
Goat   105
Goring-on-Thames, The Miller of Mansfield   48
Granby, Marquis of   114
Graysholt, The Fox and Pelican   46
Greene King brewery   79, 80
Gribble, Paul   80, 81
Guiseley, The Yorkshire Rose   131

Hand   106
Hardy, Thomas   78
Harp Alley, Shoe Lane   46
Harrison, William   23
Hart, The   106, 143
Hartley Signs Ltd., Norman   75, 76, 77, 146
Hawkes, Mike   77, 79
Hayes Common, The George and Dragon   46

Hedgehog, The   106
Hemel Hempstead, The Red Lion   112
Henri II, King   48
Henry VIII, King   13, 34, 50, 51, 92, 109
Highwayman   106
History of Signboards   85
Hobson's Choice   106
Hoddesdon, The Fish and Eels   74
Hodgson, J.E.   45, 48, 49
Hogarth, William   11, 46, 47, 48, 49, 85
Hole In The Wall, The   106
Holmfirth, The Royal Oak   132
Hood, Robin   130
Hoop, The   23, 114
Hop, The   107
Horse, The   29, 142, 143
humour on signs   48, 49, 73, 85–88, 103

Inde Coope Limited   74, 75
James I, King   15
John, Saint   134
Johnson, Ben   7
Johnson, Samuel   8
Jolly, Various   107, 139
Jones, Graham   79, 80
Katz, Solomon H.   10
Key   97, 107
King, The (various)   107, 109, 139

Labour, The   110
Lamb, The   110, 112
Lattice, The   129
Lawyer, The   85, 86, 107
Leek, The Quiet Woman   105
Leslie, C.R.   45, 48, 49
Letters, The   111
Lindsley, Kathleen M   75
Lion, The   92, 112, 116, 129
Live and Let Live, The   113
London, number of pubs   23, 34
London pub signs   22–38
London pubs
    The Angel   34, 35
    The Bleu Posts   34
    The Bolt in Tun   35

The City of Salisbury   35
The Cock   29
The Cock and Bottle   29
Elephant and Castle   35
The Haverstock Arms   155
The Hoop and Grapes   23
The Horse and Leaping Bar   29
The Jolly farmers   73
The Jolly Gardeners   35
The King's Head   33
The Nag's Head   29
The New Jolly Caulkners   38
The Old Spotted Dog   38
The Pakenham   35
The Pippinjay   29
The Queen's Head and Artichoke   33
The Running Footman   133
The Swan with the Two Necks   29
The Tabard   31
The Three Crowns   51
The Three Kings   51
The White Horse   29
The Yorkshire Gray   35
Lunways, The   113
Lute, The   113

Mackenney, George   69–72, 79, 82, 87,
    88, 103, 112
McMullens Limited   72, 73, 74
Magna Carta, The   14
Magpie, The   114
Man, various   105, 114, 113
Maria Theresa, Empress   48
materials of signs   71, 79
Maypole   114
Melton Mowbray, The Three Swans   21
Millais, Sir John Everett   46
Miller, The   100
Milton Common, The Three Pigeons   86
Milton Keynes, The Eager Poet   86
Mitre, The   114
Moon, The   114
Morland, George   39
Morland, Henry Robert   39
Mother Huff Cap, The   115

Mother Red Cap, The   115
Mother Shipton, The   115
Much Wenlock, The George and
    Dragon   104
Much Wenlock, The Talbot Inn   137
mug house   115
Museum of London, The   29, 34, 50
museums of pub signs   29, 34, 45, 50

Nag, The   115
Nails, The   90
New Inn, The   115
Nicklas, Graham   74, 75
Noah's Ark, The   135

Oak, The   115, 132
Odd One Out, The   115
Old English Gentleman, The   115
Old Parr's Head, The   116
Our Lady   116

Palm Tree, The   116
Peacock, The   116
Pelican, The   116
Penny, Edward   40
Pepys, Samuel   29, 34
Peter and Paul, The   117
Peter the Great, The   33
Pickled Egg, The   117
Piddletrenthide, The Piddle Inn   87, 117
Pig, The   85, 117
Plough, The   117
Plymouth breweries   70
Pontefract, The Chequers   98
Potters Crouch, The Holly Bush   8, 9
Prussia, King of, The   48
pub coins and tokens   16
pub signs, history of   10–18
pub signs, lifespan of   39, 48, 71
pub signs, size   16, 17, 84
pub tokens   116
pubs, history of   10–18
pubs, number of   15, 23, 34
Punch Bowl, The   24

Quart Pot, The   119
    see Tankard

railway, influence of   18, 129
Ram, The   129
Raven, The   129
religious symbols   13
    see also Adam and Eve, anchor, angel,
        fountain, hart, hole in the wall, key,
        Saint John, lamb, our lady, peacock,
        pelican, Peter and Paul, raven, rose,
        salutation, star, unicorn
Richard III, King   14, 90
Richard III, King   92
road building, influence of   18
Robin Hood, The   130
Roman influence   11, 12, 92, 97, 98
Rose The   130–32, 140
Roseneath, The Ferry Inn   48
Ross, Sir William Charles   46
Rowland, Rob   78

royal names   33

St. Martin's le Grand, The Bull and the
    Mouth   34
Saltwood, Lord Clark of   48, 49
Salutation, The   134
Saracen's Head, The   135
Saxon influence   12
Scoale, The White Hart   16, 17
sculptures (as pub signs)   35, 51
    see also wood
Shades, The   135
Shears, The   135
Ship, The   135
Sign Design Limited   74
Smith, John Thomas   33
Solihull, The Spitfire   77
Star, The   135, 136
Stilton, The Bell   20
Stokes, Thomas   22, 23
Stone, Marcus   48
Stoney Stratford, The Fox and
    Hounds   102

Stratford-upon-Avon, The
    Sportsman   78
street lights, influence of   38
Stubbs, George   72
Sudbury, The Magpie   46
Sun, The   130, 136
Swan, The   136, 143
Sword, The   136

Tabard, The   33, 136
tabernae, Roman   11, 97
Talbot, The   33, 137
Tankard, The   139
Tap, The   135
Tate Gallery, The   7
techniques in pub art   71, 75, 79
Teddington, The Teddington Hands   148
Thistle, The   139
Tinderbox, The   117
Tucker's Grave   139
Tumbledown Dick   140
Tun, The   113, 139
Turk's head, The   140
Turner, Dawson   45

Turner, J.M.W.   7

Uncle Tom, The   140
Unicorn, The   140, 141
Union, The   141

Vault(s), The   135, 141
Victoria, Queen   15, 46, 73, 88
Victoria and Albert Museum   45, 50
Vine, The   141
Vintner's Arms, The   141
Virgin
    see our lady
Vulcan, The   141
Vulture, The   142

Wagon, The   142
Wale, Samuel   40
Wales, Princess of   15
Walsall, The Pretty Bricks   118

Waltham Cross, The Four Swans   17, 18,
    19
Wargrave-on-Thames, The George and
    Dragon   45, 49
Warrenne, Earls of   11, 47, 97
Warwick, Earls of   91
Watney pubs   22, 24, 25
Websters brewery   75
Well, The   143
Wells, brewery, Charles   72
Weymouth, The Admiral Hardy   78
Wheatsheaf   143
Whistle, The   117
Whitbread, brewery   33, 77, 79, 81, 86
Whitley, The First-in Last-out   76
Whittington, Dick   144
Wildboarclough, The Cat and Fiddle   99
Wilson, Richard   39
Woman, The   129
    see also nag
wood, pub signs in   75
Woolpack, The   144
World, The   144, 145

Yarmouth, The Jolly Sailor   45
Yew tree, The   144
York, Duke of   84
York, The Olde Starre   17
York Castle museum   50

Zetland, The   144